101 Health Tips For Police Officers

HOW TO BE PHYSICALLY, MENTALLY, SPIRITUALLY, AND SOCIALLY FIT FOR DUTY

Scott Medlin

This book is a work of nonfiction. Certain names and identifying characteristics have been changed.

Front cover image by Jomari Paul Pagadua (Upwork.com)

Scott Medlin

lawenforcementmotivation@gmail.com

Foreword

As a cop, I *live* for my days off. And when I finally get to my first day off—the day that I had planned to take on the world, Walmart, the gym, and that moldy stuff in the back of the fridge—I just want to disappear in between the cushions of my couch and not come out for days. But it's so rare I ever really get a day off—between court, mandatory training, and that irresistible last-minute OT assignment, it seems like I'm always working.

Sound familiar?

Man, this job can really suck the *life* out of you. I know you know what I'm talking about. Sure, it's part of the job. But it can wear on you, and that can lead to problems.

Big problems.

Problems like compassion fatigue, exhaustion, depression, withdrawal from people, destruction of personal relationships and home life, drinking, more drinking, even suicidal thoughts or worse. We have all been affected by it, we have all seen it. We all know fellow cops who have burned out, let their personal life fall apart as they chase the job, or even worse, died by suicide because they felt they had nowhere else to turn.

We don't deserve to live like that. Our families do not deserve a mere shadow of the former person we once were. We were designed for a better quality of life. We deserve to be able to enjoy our life, our family, and our children through our law enforcement career and beyond retirement.

As a cop who has been through the darkness and overcome it, I want to share some good news with you. You *can* survive a career in law enforcement. The key to your survival is living an **actively balanced life of resilience**. Like the body armor you suit up with every day, cops need armor for their bodies, minds and hearts.

In this book, *101 Health Tips for Police Officers,* fellow police officer and author Scott Medlin gives us a real, viable list of tips and advice backed by research along with the experience of his own career and that of several veteran officers. The detailed and yet candid explanations make this an incredible resource for both rookie and veteran cops, or anyone involved in a profession or lifestyle that demands you to be 150% at all times.

As a veteran officer, I found many excellent tips in the pages ahead. Medlin's approach has great diversity and provides us with tips for physical, emotional, and spiritual survival. I have found so many things in this book to be helpful in the day to day of my career. These wellness strategies in combination with my faith in God has given me long term resilience and new purpose in serving others.

Fellow officer, deputy, trooper, dispatcher, or professional, you were meant for *more* than mundane. I want to encourage you that there is hope for you, and that the key to **not** becoming a casualty of this battle is to lead a life of resilience.

I pray that you can apply at least some of Medlin's tips to your life and your career and live the life you were given.

I will share a quote with you that always made me smile, from an old cowboy who loved police officers (who has since passed away). Whenever we would part ways, he would always say,

"Stay low in the saddle, keep off the ridges, and keep your powder dry. And if you can't—make sure you shoot straight."

God bless you,

Jonathan E. Hickory
Veteran police officer, Chaplain, and author of *Break Every Chain*
www.breakeverychainbook.com

Table of Contents

Introduction
101 Health Tips For Police Officers

It is okay, we can put all that stuffy rhetoric to the side - it is just you and me. Yes, of course you believe in "honor," "civic duty," and "making the world a better place." Of course you believe in being a positive role model for children and stopping bad guys. Still, it is also okay to just admit that policing is fun for other reasons. It does not have to be 100% altruism, because honestly, this job really can be fun and, dare I say it, even entertaining when you take the proper steps to stay healthy.

That is just the thing, though - most officers do not do enough to take care of themselves, which in this business, presents a serious problem. If you do not actively work to offset the diverse demands of this career, then you will most certainly experience health problems of one form or another. None of us are immune to it.

This book will not dive into the neurochemistry and other health concepts of the mental/physical health issues officers face, because I already covered that in _Mental Health Fight of the Heroes in Blue._

That book addresses a harrowing and heavily understated problem within the law enforcement community: officer suicide. More officers died in 2019 by their own hands than in the line of duty, and that is simply not acceptable. We have to make sure that officers understand the importance of the little things when it comes to mental and physical health, which is why that book got into the specific mechanisms of depression, addiction, and other stress-related issues.

Today, however, I am bringing you a more lighthearted, yet equally important, list of strategies and techniques you can use to fortify your mind, body, spirit, and social being against the inevitable stressors of this job. I have got 101 snippets of wisdom for you, in fact, that I drew from my own experiences, those of my colleagues, and expert opinions to create. There will also be very dynamic firsthand accounts from fellow officers and a former law enforcement spouse. The stories of these individuals are sure to open your eyes to the absolute obligation to maintain your health and well-being. We all want to be healthy, right?

I am not expecting you to memorize 101 pieces of information verbatim and create some hellishly long checklist for yourself. Instead, my hope is that you already do a few of these things, and that you can make small adjustments to accommodate as many more of these items as you can. Some techniques are more in-depth than others, but they are all important. As always, your results are a direct indication of how much work you put in.

This book is intended to be informative, but not in a dry and academic way. I have included relatable anecdotes to make it fun for you as well. I am modeling it this way for two reasons: First, I do not want you to get bored (duh). Secondly, staying healthy does not have to be boring either, so I modeled this book to reflect that. I will go ahead and apologize for the random inside jokes throughout the book that might stump and/or confuse you. Some friends/fellow officers said they would burn their copies of the book if they were not mentioned. Now back to what is important for you.

If you want to get the most out of this career instead of just going through the motions and becoming jaded, then this is your list. This is how you do better than simply staying alive. These 101 items will help you to feel happier and healthier, even when filling out felony paperwork or dealing with a rough stretch of shifts.

Apologies for the legal jargon again, but this is the part where I give you the disclaimer:

As I mentioned in *Mental Health Fight of the Heroes in Blue,* I am not a medical professional. This book does not count as treatment; it is strictly a guide based on my years of being in counseling and researching wellness and health, as well as my own experiences as an officer. Also, please read and abide by any directions and warning labels on supplements I mention in this book. Use at your own discretion and/or seek a doctor's opinion before use. In other words, it is not my fault if you drink too much colloidal silver and turn blue!

These techniques can help you, but only if you commit. It is up to you to help yourself in the end. Let the games begin!

Chapter 1
Hey Body, It Is Me: Physical Health Tips for Police Officers

It is not just about the mile time or the bench press max. Fitness is important, but *health and wellness* are not the same thing. If you really want to make some positive changes that will equip you for anything, then it's time to look at all aspects of health. And that means starting with the diet.

1. Intermittent Fasting

I know, I know, it sounds like a dumb social media trend on the surface. Some even go so far as to say that intermittent fasting is self-torture, but the truth is nothing so melodramatic. In fact, intermittent fasting is a fantastic way to burn fat, and not in the way that you are thinking.

You can still absolutely get 3 meals a day in, but now, you have an 8-hour window to do so. While you are fasting, your insulin levels drop significantly because your body does not have to worry about curbing those pesky blood sugar spikes associated with large and/or frequent meals. When insulin levels are low, your body's fatty tissue is broken down at a faster rate.

We are also finding out that serum concentrations of human growth hormone are much higher in the fasting phase as well. Do you see the potential here? Simply by sequestering your mealtime to a slightly smaller window, you help your body to both burn fat *and* build muscle!

I do not have to tell you how amazingly helpful this can be for a police officer. The movies can portray us however they want, but we know that much of the job at times is sitting on your rear end, and that does not bode well for... well, your rear end. We need all the help we can get in terms of fat reduction and muscle growth.

2. Spinach and Kale

You are not a little kid anymore. There is no spoonful of sopping, steamed spinach being "airplaned" to your mouth, so do your best to shake off that traumatized feeling when you hear these words, because it does not have to be that way. There are plenty of ways to sneak these items into your diet and/or dress them up that will satisfy even the pickiest of palates. Plus, I can confidently state that that spinach and kale will give you a clearer mind and a much less sluggish body than that giant cookie you impulsively groped for by the gas station coffee pots. Guilty as charged!

In fact, spinach and kale contain "neuroprotective" ingredients, meaning that they can armor your brain against attack from serious diseases. Even people who already have dementia, Alzheimer's, or general cognitive decline can slow the progression of these processes with the nutrients found in spinach and kale.

Remember, you are in a safe space. You are a big boy or girl now, and nobody's spoon-feeding you. You can throw in a small dab of butter with it if you want. Just get those greens in there!

3. Conquer the "Department Snacks" Wheel of Temptation

It is the same old story. You want to be good. You are trying really hard to be good. Me too! But something about the neurochemistry of unexpected, FREE snacks being shoved in your face is just simply too much for many of us officers.

Often, these snacks are donated by community members. I am not advocating at all that you decline them publicly, of course, because that is **not** an awesome way to return such a well-intended gesture. Since these snacks are usually salty, sweet, fattening, or all of the above, however, it is your job to conquer this wheel of temptation.

Here is a little advice I use for just such an occasion. *Expect* the snacks to be there. Know that they are coming and prepare yourself *before* your eyes and nose are bombarded by the sights and smells that make you salivate. If the snacks are actually there when you walk in, you will be ready. If they are not, you will have one less thing to push yourself through that day.

Another technique, chipped in by the venerable *Les Brown,* so you know it is good, is to actually practice and emphasize the act of refusing the treats. You may look and feel crazy at first, but hear me out. Walk in, see the snacks, leave the room without touching them, and repeat. It is just like a workout for your willpower. The more you do it, the better you will be in the future.

Combine these two methods and practice them regularly, and you will overcome the department snacks wheel of temptation for sure!

4.   Ixnay on the Late Meals and Snacks

Hate to say it, but even if *what* you are eating is semi-healthy, *when* you eat it can drastically affect metabolism for better or worse. It may seem the natural thing to do - falling asleep after a big meal - but this kind of sentiment does not bode well for your health in real life.

When you eat right before going to bed, your body has to spend a lot of energy in those initial hours of sleep digesting that meal or even snack. This means that your ability to enter a restful state is compromised, or at the very least, distracted.

Even if you simply cannot bring yourself to jump on the intermittent fasting wagon (seriously, the water's fine), then at least try eating early enough to give yourself more than three hours of awake time for digestion. I am not even saying you have to wolf down boiled cabbage and lentils every meal - just eating earlier is a great baby step into a healthier diet.

By "healthier," I do mean in terms of weight loss - not just longevity. Eating early enough and allowing your body the opportunity to digest means that you can get a serious head start on not just absorbing the fats and other nutrients, but putting them to use (instead of storing them).

5. Stretch!

Flexibility is woefully, I say **woefully** underappreciated part of so many fitness routines. In fairness, athletes tend to be more vigilant about stretching because of savvy coaches. However, this massive resurgence we have seen in the popularity of "deadlifting, bro" culture is totally remiss to stretching. The "bro" was for Dover.

Keeping your muscles flexible, long, and lean "equals youth," as one of my fitness instructors, *Sean Vigue*, likes to say. Many of us follow this weird misconception that, if you are not in agonizing pain because you just pulled a hamstring or strained your back, then you do not need to stretch.

The truth is not so convenient. Your muscles and the fascial layer that covers them will absolutely twist, shorten, develop toxic metabolites (knots), and pull at your bones until your posture is so out of place that you look like Quasimodo.

Then comes the neck pain, back pain, vertebral malalignments, headaches, weakness, and the beer gut to match it. This is *guaranteed* if you do not stretch regularly. It is not just about preparing for a workout, but optimizing your postural mechanics so you can work, live, eat, play with your kids, sleep, and you know, live without pain.

Stretch your ever-loving self!! You might just feel relieved.

6. Exercise

I tried to beat around the bush a bit, but come on - we both knew this was coming. I will make sure to dive more into the specifics later, but for now, let us just start with the idea of exercising.

I could write an entire book as it relates specifically to the importance of exercise for law enforcement folks. There are so, so, so many ways to exercise. Some of the ways to exercise are wrong and many of them right. There is honestly no excuse to not commit to at least a moderately challenging program.

The good news is this: just twenty minutes to an hour on alternating days will be enough to maintain a healthy fitness level if you actually push yourself (Instead of just yakking with fellow gym-goers while leaning on the equipment).

Most people are well aware of the long-established correlation between exercise and cardiovascular health. There is muscle tone and development, balance, and so forth, but many understate the importance of exercise for your mental health.

Technically, when you workout, you are inflicting pain on yourself. It is in a controlled, healthy setting, but it is still pain. Your body responds with substances called enkephalins and endorphins. Your body's response to exercise is not "like" a drug, it *is* a drug - and it helps your attitude and mental health just as much as it helps your body.

For now, I will say this: As long as you are safe, short and intense is better than two hours at a tortoise's pace. Of course you are busy - we all are. Push yourself hard enough, and you can be "wrapping up the final fifteen minutes" of your workout as soon as you start - just look at it that way!

For example, I learned an amazing pushup workout from Marine Corps (retired) Sergeant Major Courville during my time at the USMC Officer Candidate School in Quantico, VA. The workout was simple. Do 400 push-ups in twenty minutes. That is twenty push-ups a minute, and you start exactly on the minute. Whatever time you have left until the next minute is rest. To clarify, you do not do twenty and then rest a full minute. Join the 400 Club!!

Disclaimer: Always stretch to avoid injury, and use your own good judgment when determining which exercises are best for you - not as an excuse to wuss out!

7. Yoga

Remember all that talk about stretching and youthfulness? One of the most incredible delivery systems for an intense, well-rounded, and posture-minded stretching sessions is definitely yoga. Sure, you could hem and haw all you want out of insecurity, like I used to do, but then I decided I would rather feel better than care what other people think.

Yoga is more than five millennia old, and it is still here. That means something. It has helped people all over the world conquer more than just muscle tightness. If you really drink the kool-aid and get into meditative breathing, chakras, etc., you will be amazed at just how deep this rabbit hole goes in terms of health benefits.

For example, the American Osteopathic Association lists the benefits of yoga as:

-increased flexibility
-increased muscle strength and tone
-improved respiration, energy, and vitality
-balanced metabolism
-weight loss
-cardio and circulatory health
-improved athletic performance
-protection from injury
-stress management

Even if you are not a fan of the hippy-dippy veneer surrounding yoga (no offense, my fellow yogis!), it is no reason to shut yourself off from this incredibly effective workout. And oh yeah, it is definitely a workout if you have never tried it before. Do not believe me? Try it.

8. Weightlifting

Make no mistake, strength is a requirement if you want to meet some of the most important demands of the job, like deterring a criminal from fighting, overcoming a criminal when it does happen, keeping a tight grip during arrest procedures, and simply bearing the weight of your uniform. Weightlifting is not just about looking tough or even being strong, however. According to a PoliceMag *article* by Deputy Whitney Richtmyer and Will Brink, weightlifting also helps to increase your bone density, which brings forward a number of helpful benefits:

-Greater resistance to injury/fracture in the event of a hard impact
-Improved ability to fight off stress-related injuries from poor posture or repeated physical encounters in the field

You do not need to be throwing up 450 on the bench to make this happen, either. Not every officer has a bodybuilder's frame, and that is okay. Simply cranking out a few standing push presses can help build strength and ward off those pesky postural deficiencies. Even if you do not have a ton of extra gear (gun, magazines, radio, and handcuffs only), it is still vital to work on this. There is simply no getting around the requirement of maintaining at least a moderate strength level. You owe it to yourself and your loved ones.

9. Deep Breathing

Every cell in your body and brain does its job much better with a generous supply of oxygen. In fact, your brain is such a heavy consumer of oxygen- and nutrient-rich blood, it only takes a few minutes without oxygen to sustain serious damage or complete cell death. According to *Wim Hof,* the undisputed master of breathing and cold therapy, most of us are too shallow in our breathing. We are getting enough oxygen to stay alive, but not enough for our cells to perform optimally. And since cells do, well, everything, that is no small problem.

Without sufficient oxygen, our natural equilibrium gets thrown off in all kinds of ways, on the level of hormones and otherwise. This shortage affects immunity, energy, attitude, strength, and a whole lot more.

Most of us are chest breathers. It sounds funny at first, but deep and healthy respiration is actually a product of "stomach breathing." Here is how you test yourself to determine which one you are: First, lay flat on your bed or the floor (floor is actually more accurate). Place one hand on your chest and the other on your stomach. Take a few deep breaths in and out. Which one, chest or stomach, experienced a greater rise and fall? Again, for most of us, it is our chest, but it is supposed to be the stomach. Condition yourself to expand your stomach on the inhalation and flatten it back in on the exhalation. This small change is great for your overall health in the long run, but even better when you are on a high-stress call.

10. Walking

You heard me - walking. Whether you are riding a desk or patrolling the streets at 0300 on a rainy night, you may find yourself sitting for a long period of time. I simply cannot emphasize this enough - this is an awful habit that far too many of us get into. Prolonged sitting can lead to a ton of cardiovascular, gastrointestinal, and other issues, including deep vein thrombosis (DVT or blood clots), diverticulitis, cancer, and more. Walking less and sitting more is one of my greatest regrets during the several years I was on patrol. Too often I found myself feeling achy and stiff after a shift - I was doing more damage than I knew.

In addition to the physical benefits, walking has meditative, calming effects on your mind. If you are just staring at your phone, not so much; not only could you trip and hurt yourself (LOL!), but you are not giving your mind that break.

It is vital that you walk as often as you can during your shifts. Everything in our bodies was made to move, and when you sit for too long, bad things happen. Worst case scenario in the short-term is that you pull a hamstring or get a cramp when chasing after or subduing a suspect.

11. Chlorella and Spirulina Algae

Go ahead, take a minute to digest what appears to be a round of Scrabble. No, it is not chlorine and spiral noodles - Chlorella and Spirulina algae. I had not heard about these two substances until 2018. I was suffering from a number of health issues and fortunately my brother informed me about these two green prodigies of nature.

Sure enough, just days into my regimen, I felt much better. Chlorella and Spirulina are antioxidant-rich supplements dense in vitamins, minerals, and proteins - many of which we do not get enough of in our diets.

Antioxidants are substances that exert "neuroprotective" effects on the cells in our brains as well as the tissues in our body. These are especially relevant today because of the ridiculously high number of free radical (unstable cells that cause damage to healthy cells by ripping off electrons) sources in today's society, e.g., fried foods and junk food, stress, and even just standing there while radio waves pass through you! Try going on *that* diet - not possible.

Of course, these supplements are not a green light for you to shovel in as much junk food as possible - that would pretty much negate the positive effects. If you maintain a healthy diet in the meantime, however, you will be able to detox your liver and other cells to great effect.

Remember to read any warning labels and instructions!!

12. Zinc and Magnesium

It is easy to neglect the importance of trace nutrients like zinc and magnesium when it comes to our health routines for a few reasons. First, it is hard for us to relate. I mean, protein, fat, and carbs we know, but *zinc and magnesium*? What are we, robots? Secondly, since they are trace elements, we do not need nearly as much of these as we do the crowd-pleasers like protein, fat, etc., but the trade-off is that they already exist in such low concentrations in food.

The health merits of both nutrients are not even debatable, however. You definitely do not want to take too much zinc or magnesium, because too much of a good thing is rarely a good thing, but calculated supplementation is needed for most of us. Zinc and magnesium are vital for immune system function, thyroid function, muscle performance, and more.

Thankfully, zinc is not that commonly underconsumed in America especially, as it is found in red meat (and spinach if you do not eat meat), but magnesium often goes ignored. You can find magnesium in almonds, pumpkin seeds, cashews, spinach (hey, 2 for 1!), raisins, and a few other foods, though, so there is no excuse!

13. Vitamin C

The problem with Vitamin C is that many adults fallaciously believe that it is no longer important after you are a kid, or at least not as important. We ram it down childrens' throats, both metaphorically and literally, in hopes that they will have at least some ammunition as they unwittingly plunge headfirst into the battlefield of germs that is school or daycare. But adults need Vitamin C too!

Yes, Vitamin C is especially helpful for immune protection, growth and development. It also holds many applications for adults of all ages, including continued immune support and even dental health.

Point being, it is still vital for you to maintain healthy levels of Vitamin C, and not just in a seasonal way. Taking Vitamin C should not be seen as a temporary treatment to fend off illness, but a permanent practice to maintain overall health.

Thankfully, Vitamin C is somewhat omnipresent in terms of the number of common foods that contain it, including broccoli, spinach (seriously, guys and girls, spinach is your friend), fruits, and yes, pills and supplements.

When you do not consume enough Vitamin C, you may notice it in energy levels, frequent illness, damaged or easily bruised skin, and more. It is always better to source your nutrients with the "carrier nutrients" they were born next to, i.e., in the form of food, but if that is simply not enough, then supplements are much better than nothing.

14. Vitamin D

Fun fact for the day - did you know that Vitamin D is actually not a vitamin? It did not take too long into the research findings for me to learn that factoid. Thanks to Dr. Debra Sullivan's article on Medical News Today, I learned that vitamin D is not considered a vitamin because it can be synthesized by the body, where true vitamins cannot (which is why we have to source them from food and supplements).

To avoid discombobulation, I will still refer to this substance as Vitamin D. You probably know that the body needs sunlight to create Vitamin D, but this comes with the obvious trade-off of the perils of prolonged sun exposure.

As to its function, Vitamin D is vital in immune system health, bone density, gut health, and more.

In addition to sunlight, you can still source Vitamin D from food, although this will be an uphill battle from the start if you hardly ever go outside. Vitamin D can be found in egg yolks, beef liver, salmon, mushrooms, and other foods. In the case of Vitamin D deficiency, you are likely to experience skin problems, energy level problems, immune system deficiencies (which manifests in about a hundred other problems), and more. The best practice to ensure adequate levels is to simply get an annual checkup and/or have a blood test taken for Vitamin D and other nutrients.

15. B Vitamins

Among the majority of vitamins that your body does not produce, i.e., the kind that you have to exclusively seek out in food, is vitamin B. If you feel sluggish, or if you feel one of those people who eats well and exercises without seeing results, then your metabolism may very well be in play.

This is primarily where Vitamin B shines - it greatly bolsters your metabolism so that your body can break down compounds in food and actively convert them to energy (ideal) or stored fat (important to an extent, but should be second place to energy).

To avoid confusion, B vitamins go by other names that you have likely heard of: folic acid, riboflavin, B12, and niacin. Keep these levels steady, and you will establish much greater energy levels, easier weight loss and muscle growth, and a host of additional benefits like hormone balancing and reduced risk of stroke.

"That's all good and fine," you may be saying to yourself, "but do I have to eat lentil and boiled cabbage all day now?" Thankfully, the culinary landscape is not so grim when it comes to B vitamins; there are plenty of tasty foods you can find that will kick in a generous shot of the above nutrients, including:

-Chicken, turkey, pork
-Yogurt
-Fortified cereal
-Trout
-Sunflower seeds
-Nutritional and brewer's yeast

(Data obtained from HealthLine.com)

See? Not so terrible.

16. Martial Arts

Boy, has Hollywood ever done a number on this one. Most people, no offense, are almost completely ignorant as to the true benefits of martial arts. Yes, you can learn hand-to-hand defensive tactics that will give you the edge you need in a physical encounter with a criminal. Obviously, that is a very, very high priority safety item when it comes to law enforcement officials, so I do not mean to de-emphasize that.

However, just like yoga and deep breathing, martial arts also introduces a ton of time-tested meditation techniques and movement patterns that support mental well-being, calmness, and more. It also enhances "proprioception," which is a fancy word for your awareness of where your body is in space (if you close your eyes and raise your hand, how do you know your hand is there?). Proprioception is a very helpful skill when it comes to both fighting as well as maintaining a healthy posture.

It is important to note that officers are encouraged to train in a form of martial arts that lines up with the defensive tactics we are taught. For example, learning to roundhouse kick someone in the face (as in Taekwondo and other Kung Fu styles) is not exactly applicable to the practical submission techniques we learn. Especially nowadays, this practice will not bode well for you.

Alternatively, Brazilian Jiu Jitsu and Aikido are both focused on quick and efficient submission techniques that do not require you to strike someone, which is better for everyone involved - you and the criminal. I also found that through training in Krav Maga, you can learn multiple techniques from control and restraint, to defending against multiple attackers.

17. Herbal Tea

Here is a hilarious meme: "All officers are required to report to the next SWAT briefing with a cup of naturally sourced herbal tea."

Look, I get it. Herbal tea is about as "granola sounding," if not more so, than the idea of yoga, meditation, deep breathing, etc.

All kidding aside, however, if you read *Mental Health Fight of the Heroes in Blue,* then you know just how stressful this occupation can be on both body and mind. To refuse something that could directly counteract these stressors in a natural and affordable way, then, is to really shoot yourself in the foot. The less stressed you are, the healthier you are. This means improved immunity and energy levels for that fight that could break out any minute.

Tea has been around for a very, very long time, so it has lost a bit of its "zing" in terms of marketing buzz (not as sexy or exciting as mega fat burner XX elite whatever), but that does not mean it is not helpful. It still aids greatly in creating a sense of calm, improving digestion, fat burning/detox, and much more.

As always, it is indeed possible to drink too much tea, as some people are in the habit of doing - especially those trying to wean themselves off of coffee. I know you are trying hard to be good and your intentions are pure, but try to keep it to two cups a day.

As to the kind, you do not need to be super picky, so long as it is a natural herbal tea: chamomile, turmeric, green, ginger, and even peppermint. It is all good!

18. Colloidal Silver

Admittedly, we have approached a bit of a fine line. I am compelled to tell you that the FDA does not recognize that colloidal silver is beneficial in any way, but that does not mean the substance is harmful.

Yes, there are risks involved with taking any non-FDA-regulated supplement (and even regulated ones), but the lack of regulation just means that more research is required. To be frank, it could mean that it is not politically advantageous for the FDA to go down this avenue at this time (I mean, just look at CBD).

Either way, there is a growing body of evidence affirming the health benefits of colloidal silver. It has been shown to boost the effects of antibiotics, and it facilitates immune function when you are not sick as well. Colloidal silver is indicated for a vast field of conditions, and in my case, greatly alleviates problems like colds.

Again, it is completely up to you to take this non-regulated supplement, and as always, I highly recommend you do your research and/or consult with a physician. If you do decide to take it, do not worry - you do not have to find some guy in an alleyway to get it. Simply head to your local vitamin shop.

19. Elderberry

It has been a popular staple of grocery store end caps and commercial spots for some time now, but that does not mean elderberry is not the real deal. In fact, this is one of the few over-marketed health "gimmicks" that does actually work in more ways than one.

In his YouTube video entitled "*Elderberry vs Illness - Does It Help?*" fitness and nutrition expert *Thomas DeLauer* breaks down several of the life-affirming qualities of elderberry products. He cites a study conducted by the *Journal of International Medical Research* to validate his claims. This is what the study said, per DeLauer's video:

In a group of 60 patients aged 18-54 who were suffering from influenza-like symptoms, 15 ml of elderberry syrup administered 4 times a day for 5 days showed improved symptoms in 2 to 4 days (as opposed to 7 to 8 days for the control group).

If I may echo this recurring theme once more, Thomas also goes on to point out that you should not use elderberry every day. This strikes at the heart of the "essential nutrients vs supplements" issue. In the case of vitamins that our bodies do not produce, we of course have to always be seeking those out in food. By constantly propping up our existing immunity with supplements, however, we run the risk of becoming deficient when those supplements are removed. Your body just says, *well, I guess I can produce less xyz now that we are getting so much of it.*

20. Sleep

You probably saw this one coming from a mile away, and for good reason. Sleep is absolutely imperative for more reasons than one - especially in law enforcement. You may be able to muddle through a shift in the cubicle with less than optimal sleep however unpleasant it may be to you. In our world though, the stakes are much higher.

Simply put, if you feel groggy and unmotivated, it is likely that your body is trying to tell you something about sleep. At the very least, you should be getting seven to eight hours a night (or day if you work the night shift).

As I covered in *Mental Health Fight of the Heroes in Blue,* post traumatic stress disorder, depression, and anxiety are all closely correlated with sleep. This is an inverse correlation between severity of symptoms and sleep, meaning the closer to seven to eight hours you get, the better you will feel mentally.

Here is how: get a handle on your distractions, turn off all your electronics at least thirty minutes before bed, stretch, and actively remind yourself that you are not in danger. You are off work, you and your family are safe, and it is okay to shut down. These methods will work together to facilitate your brain's production of melatonin and other helpful sleep chemicals. This means more deep and consistent sleep, which also means:

-Mood disorder prevention
-Renewed motivation
-Short-term and long-term memory preservation
-Renewed ability to focus
-Decreased workload for the heart and other organ

systems
-Immune system repair

I could go on and on and on, but you get the gist! Now for one of my favorites...

21. Get Outside!

The benefits of spending some quality time with the outdoors are just about innumerable. For one, you get that Vitamin D synthesis machine going, which will help with your skin, mood, immune system, and much more.

There is also a more subjective element at play here that transcends the science a bit, even crossing over into the spiritual/existential self. I will not go on rambling about the spirituality of it all, but I am not the only one who believes that going outside is just plain old good for the soul.

In terms of your cognitive acuity, going outside (especially as part of a hunting/fishing excursion or a sport) can be really helpful for your brain health. For thousands upon thousands of years, mankind roamed around in the wilds fending for himself, and our brains have not quite updated themselves to this post-industrial landscape. My point is that completing tasks outside helps to exercise our base problem-solving abilities and instincts in a way that helps maintain brain health.

In general, getting out of that recycled air and letting some sunlight hit your skin while you get some exercise is just a triple whammy at the very least.

22. Get a Standing Desk

More specifically, an adjustable desk that comfortably accommodates both sitting and standing positions. Now, I understand what your reply may be upon hearing this recommendation. "Scott, I'm in a patrol car all day!" All it takes is a bit of resourcefulness to mitigate this issue. When it is time to complete your reports, set your laptop on the trunk of your car, turn off the engine to save gas (and your lungs), and there you have it! Roger?

As mentioned in my other book, sitting really is the new smoking. Being down for prolonged periods of time is bad for you on almost every level (weight gain, joint health, cardio health, immunity, mental health, etc.)

Granted, even if you could stand for eight hours, that would definitely not be smart for your feet, knees, etc. It is okay to sit for a few minutes at a time, just not all day. Stand up as often as you can. You will burn more calories, exercise your postural muscles, nourish the cartilage in your joints, breathe more deeply and openly, and much, much more.

23. Chair Yoga

Just because you saw grandma doing this in the nursing home does not mean it is only for old folks. On the contrary, chair yoga is an excellent way to get a bit of exercise and keep your circulation up for those of us who do have to sit for most of the day.

You do not have to be sweating bullets (many of us already are with all the gear and the heat). All I am talking about here is a few simple stretches that you can complete in a sitting position and on a rotating basis. For example, spinal twists are a great start. You can also lift one cheek off the chair at a time as you tilt your core from side to side in an alternating fashion, which will work those quadratus/oblique muscles in your back while giving the blood vessels on your rear end a bit of a breathing break. In addition, you can stretch your shoulders, traps, neck, hamstrings, and more from a seated position.

This is just the tip of the iceberg, mind you. There are dozens upon dozens of stretches you can do in a seated position. I recommend you devise a routine of rotating stretches and perform them often enough so that they become a habit. It is also pertinent to note that you should never compromise your driving safety to get these stretches in, of course, so modify as needed.

24. Postural Training

Many of us cannot help but give a compulsory eye-roll at the mention of postural training because it brings us back to our adolescent years of being harped on by mom, dad, or whoever else. As usual, though, they were right. Maintaining a strong posture is not only good for your spine and the rest of your body, but it can even affect your mood.

Most people would not debate that posture is generally good, but even more people are just too locked into their routines to integrate postural awareness. Look at it this way - we learn in interview and interrogation classes that the body does not lie, right? If someone is slouching and hanging their head, they are clearly distressed, meaning they are either very upset and/or attempting to lie to you, strategically omit certain truths, or manipulate you in another way.

Our posture is a reflection of our mood, so when you report to a call, if you have your shoulders and chin back and your chest out (reasonably, not like a rooster), you exude a sense of confidence and trustworthiness. Just a tiny bit helpful in the law enforcement world, wouldn't you think?

There are hundreds of postural cues we could review, but I will wrap this point up with the most needed issues. As mentioned, you will want to squeeze the muscles between your shoulder blades so that the shoulders are not rounded forward (they are pulled back) and your chest sticks out a little bit instead of being caved in. Also, practice chin tucks and cervical retractions (moving your head backwards so that your chin comes back) to fight that forward head posture we all get from staring at screens all day. These little tricks alone will literally save you a ton of pain.

25. Smile - Yes, Smile

Everyone has heard the old adage about apples and doctors, but I have a similar permutation for you. "A smile a day keeps the negativity away." Now, you do not have the luxury of walking away from negative people as a law enforcement officer, but you can still practice this within your friend group. Ironically, smiling is seen as a sign of weakness, but in reality, the ability to smile in the face of adversity is the mark of a strong stoic. It means that even the toughest of situations, you are strong enough to be calm, cool, and even happy.

This is arguably a mental health item, but since smiling is a physical act, I have decided to sneak it into this category. Plus, it really is exceptionally beneficial for your physical health. Of course, I am not saying that you should smile when approaching a dangerous criminal, but when you are working with scared, traumatized, or otherwise distressed people, a smile can indeed go a long way.

According to a NeuroNation article, smiling is a signal to your brain that you feel healthy, which catalyzes a number of helpful neurochemical processes. Here is a quote from the piece:

"When a smile flashes across your face, dopamine, endorphins, and serotonin are all released into your bloodstream, making not only your body relax but also work to lower your heart rate and blood pressure."

Help yourself out and smile whenever it is appropriate to do so. Even if you do not feel like it. Eventually, and this is the most miraculous part, you will.

*****

My name is Matt and I am grateful to have grown up in a supportive family within a tight knit community. Throughout those caring years, I had a positive outlook on life and the hand that it deals each individual. As I started reaching my formidable teenage/young adult years, I believed that a profession in public service would allow me to serve as a chief contributor to keeping the world positive. I also regarded it as a way to help those who were most in need.

After earning my Bachelor of Science in criminal justice, I landed my first law enforcement job in 2004. I was ecstatic! I hit the ground running, working nonstop to make a difference in any way possible. I was unrelenting in my efforts to solve marital issues on the domestic calls, to help out kids who were in abusive homes, and support those battling substance abuse. There were obviously many more aspects of the job and I stayed focused on that job, not how I felt.

I would like to fast forward to 2010. I had lovingly married my longtime girlfriend. I was a husband and I was crazy about my wife. I also continued to work as a police officer. I was doing the same thing I had done in the profession for years, and unfortunately, I began to notice deviations in my physical and mental health.

After a full twelve-hour work shift, I had no desire at all to share the negativity with my wife at home. I held the gruesome crime scenes and horrific sights of violence, internally. I never considered taking time to depend on the support that my wife or other family members would have gladly given to me. I felt embarrassed to utilize employee programs such as Employee Assistance Program (EAP). My blood pressure skyrocketed, and I began to drink heavily. In addition to all of that, I started to take antidepressants on a daily basis. Still, these issues would not cause me to swallow my masculine pride and seek help.

In 2017 my drinking had aggressively continued, my stress levels were frighteningly high, and my marriage was suffering horribly. Instead of talking about the days' events and how I felt, I became very hateful to those in my personal life. It was an unintended consequence and regular occurrence. I purposely pushed those who cared about me away, in order to avoid sharing my years of buried emotional damage. In 2018, an appointment to the doctor revealed that I had developed type two diabetes, an over worked liver, and strained kidneys.

I was shocked. How could this happen to me? I landed the job I desired, and the stress of it started to kill me and I had no idea. I became devasted, and really considered if it was worth living in such a miserable state of health. I actually weighed the pros and cons of suicide. I even pondered the effects suicide would have had on my family and the result it would have on my soul.

After fiercely fighting this battle inside of myself, I made my choice to make changes in all aspects of my life. The first thing I decided to do was speak to my doctor about what could be done for me medically. I opened up about how all of those years of being closed off about the job had taken a gigantic toll on me. I allowed the guidance to prompt me to quickly cut out alcohol completely from my life, and replace it with fulfilling activities and family interaction. I also utilized medical leave from work which was highly recommended by my doctor.

*After making these changes, I have totally reformed my health, both mental and physical. Sure, there are still days that are hard, but I keep in mind that they are temporary. Please consider that tomorrow will be better if you stay on the right path and continue to work on yourself **daily**. Remember, these battles inside of you should be looked at as a deadly force situation. The mental and physical sickness that we experience can be as deadly as a suspect's bullet, if it is left unchecked. Utilize the methods in this book, continuously learn how to help yourself get through the stress of this job, and take action. Also, never become closed off from the great people who are around you. If things are falling apart, please never forget that you can change for the better.*

-Master Police Officer Matt Urps

Chapter 2
Your Mental Health Is Paramount

We as law enforcement officers are socially pressured to remain stoic and unaffected when exposed to traumatic situations. This creates a really unhealthy cycle when it comes to preserving mental health. If something that happens in the field affects you, you feel like you cannot talk about it because you are "not supposed to be affected by it." So you bottle it up inside, which leads to PTSD, depression, anxiety, and as I covered previously, even self-harm and suicide.

Let me be the first (or hopefully, not the first) to tell you that it is *okay* to feel overwhelmed or upset. It is okay to cry, talk to someone about your traumatic experiences, and work through those responses instead of just bottling them up. These steps will facilitate this process so you can best address your unique mental health needs.

1. Choose to be happy

I am really not trying to be tedious here - the subjective art of achieving happiness starts with a voluntary choice. For example, even outside the world of policing, there are types of people we all know who believe they will not be happy until they get that house, car, or vacation, and there are others who just need a chair and a fishing rod, whether or not they can afford their mortgage. Happiness is not realized from external factors, but internal. It is up to you to make the choice.

Take a look at _Nick Vujicic_, for goodness sakes. This man was born with no arms and no legs, yet he has used his unique situation and his relentlessly positive outlook on life to motivate millions of people across the world.

Public ridicule was a track that looped for most of Vujicic's childhood, to the extent were he even attempted suicide. This was his rock bottom. Instead of continuing to wallow, he used it as an opportunity to follow the path God laid out for him and dedicate his life to inspiring others.

Point being, you can actually *shape* your own state, and in turn, your future. It is a really powerful force once you learn to tap into it - the choice to appreciate what you have, be happy, and forward that gift unto others. It is okay to be depressed once in a while, but if you get into a pattern of self-victimization or anger as a result, then it is time to embrace this idea of choosing happiness.

2. Meditate

The perfect example of "do not bash it if you have not tried it," meditation is an absolute game changer, no matter where you are in your journey. I myself used to laugh at the idea of sitting there and "doing nothing." Especially in a super capitalistic, and quite frankly, materialistic country like the USA, the idea of *not working* on something and *not* worrying about bills seems unproductive.

"But you are just sitting there. Cool story, BRUH."

Look - in order to appreciate meditation, we have to make a brief departure from our Western mindset and dabble ever so slightly in Eastern philosophy. Meditation helps you to quiet yourself. It allows you to transcend your lower-level thought processes (what will I make for dinner, what is on TV tonight, etc.) and instead focus on deeper subconscious thought patterns. According to Dr. Joe Dispenza, the meditation expert, "The subconscious is where all your bad habits and behaviors you want to change reside."

In other words, meditation is like rebooting your computer. It clears all the "windows" you had open, takes a break, and jumpstarts your mind with renewed focus. And by the way, if you still feel like meditation is for hitchhiking hippies, then maybe you can ask Oprah, Jerry Seinfeld, Hugh Jackman, and Steph Curry what they think about it!

3. Skip the morning phone check

It is so, so, so easy to overlook. That is the thing about checking your phone in the morning, or at any time of the day. The threshold of effort is just so low. Just pop it out, check it, and put it back in your pocket. Done. Five seconds.

But this is much more harmful to your productivity and peace of mind than it may seem. According to a study by IDC Research, at least 80% of smartphone users (the 10 flip phone users out there do not count) check their phone within the first fifteen minutes of waking up. According to StudyFinds, 1 in 4 adults will check their phone within the first *minute!*

The neuropsychology behind this bad habit is startling to say the least. From the very first minute of your day, checking your phone places you in a less productive mindset. I could write an entire book on this issue alone, but just know for now that we all need to break this habit. I stated we because I am no exception.

If you still think I am overreacting, just do me a favor and try it out. It is not about the five seconds you save not checking your phone, but the *state of mind* you preserve by not doing so. Without the frivolous and/or negative news, social media dribble, and other information clogging up your head space, you will be that much more prepared to take on the day.

4. Wake up to something uplifting

I am following up #3 with this point for a reason - this is what you can replace your impulsive morning phone check with. Instead of checking your phone and letting the negative stream wash over you, listen to something uplifting instead.

It does not have to be some roided-up bodybuilder screaming at you to get your worthless self out of bed. In fact, that may produce the opposite effect. It just has to inhabit a positive place in your mind. Even if it is just a sounds of nature track, then fine. If you do love to be pushed and motivated, however, you absolutely can let *Jocko Willink* hype you up for a few minutes.

Your mind is more susceptible to suggestion when you first wake up, meaning those first few messages you hear carry a greater impact that can drive you through your entire day. If you listen to something positive, then, you are greatly increasing your chances of having a great day by *making it* a great day, not just passively hoping that things around you fall together.

That is the distinction that lives at the heart of this little tip. If you ditch the phone and replace it with something uplifting, you are taking control of your day instead of walking in, unprepared and just hoping you are dealt a good hand. Heck, I am listening to focus music right now, and listened to the "Hip-Hop Preacher" *Dr. Eric Thomas* to start my day.

5. The 30-day no-news challenge

"Scott, you are crazy."

Indeed, I know that refraining from checking the news sounds a little bit crazy. Of course it is important to feel connected to society. Of course it is important to stay up to date on current events and contribute to topical conversations.

But when is the last time the mainstream media provided those opportunities for you?

I am not interested in getting political **at all.** Really. But whichever side of the line you fall on, I think most of us agree that the American mainstream media is banking on appealing to our basest and most primitive instincts to keep ratings up. Instead of objectively informing us, they are trying to shock us, anger us, and divide us with sneaky rhetoric, image manipulation, and other tactics.

If you do not believe me, just take two minutes to reflect the next time you sit down to your news feed. How do you feel?

This is what I propose. Refrain from checking any and all news feeds, articles, or other content for 30 days, but assign a friend of yours as a "spotter." This way, if anything absolutely crucial happens that you must know about, your friend can report that for you.

Senator x's sexting scandal and celebrity y's triggered Twitter rant are not going to help you clear your head space. They are not going to help you with your depression, anxiety, fatigue, or whatever else you may be dealing with.

Let me put it this way. I want you to pull yourself out of this toxic cycle and watch from a much, much farther distance. The peace this brings you will be almost immeasurable, but like so many things in life, it is the slow and "unsexy" version instead of the "OMG can you believe person X said thing Y?!" scenario. The former leads to lasting peace, and the latter just keeps us sucked into the negativity. We deal with enough negativity in the job! Ok I am getting heated! Take a deep breath with me. In for four seconds, hold it forever, I mean four seconds, and then out for four seconds. Moving on now.

6. Write down what you are grateful for

Gratitude is absolutely essential to happiness. Even the richest person in the world will be outdone by someone eventually. It is *impossible,* literally impossible, to find happiness in material things. When you are grateful for what little you have, then you have found the only way to win the rat race.

But gratitude is an exercise, not an innate ability. The more you voice it, the stronger its positive influence will be in your life. That is why I want you to actually write down what you are grateful for. Do not think about it or even say it - just write it down. You can repeat it and meditate on it afterwards.

Write down three things that you are grateful for in the morning and three more in the evening. This exercise is essential for law enforcement officers especially, because it helps pull you out of that "Survive! Survive! Death is everywhere, keep the head on a swivel!" mentality.

When I was battling depression, this technique was instrumental in overcoming it. Gratitude safeguards you against the inevitable challenges of life. When you get knocked down, your gratitude will remind you that you are not down there by yourself. You still have that special person, or your family, or your health, or whatever else you are grateful for.

7. Surround yourself with positive music and podcasts

If the audio content you surround yourself with on a daily basis is the neurological equivalent to a fast food diet, then can you really be surprised when you become mentally sluggish, negative, and unproductive?

I would be the last one to deprive you of your culture, or to judge your experiences and preferences in life, but there is a line here. On one side is awesome and uplifting music, which can be found in every culture, but on the other side is profane and hateful music that objectifies people, glorifies violence, and so on, which can also be found in most cultures.

My point is that you can still enjoy the style of music you like, no matter what style it is, without the hate and negativity. What you listen to informs how you feel. Listen to sad music, and your brain will release "sad chemicals." Listen to negative music, and the same happens.

In addition to keeping your musical influences positive, I have found great inspiration, solace, and amusement in podcasts, many of which are free nowadays. You can learn a ton of actually useful concepts in podcasts that will help you enrich your family life, financial well-being, mental and spiritual health, and much more.

8. Check emails at 11:00 and 3:00

Seems oddly specific, I know, but there is a calculated method in play here. In his book *Eat That Frog,* world-renowned speaker and author *Brian Tracy* breaks down just how incredibly harmful email-checking can be in terms of time management and productivity.

"Wait a second Scott, we are talking about work emails here! Not social media."

And "boom goes the dynamite". There is the problem. See, today, email-checking flies under the radar when it comes to practices we seek to streamline for productivity purposes because they are deemed essential for work.

Yes, emails are essential for many of us who communicate with other people and departments, but that does not mean you have to check it every 3 minutes. There is a healthy balance here, and it is important to set the standard early on in your workplace relationships so that people understand you will not neurotically reply to every email within three minutes.

Check your emails at 11:00 and 3:00 every day, reply to them all in two waves, and watch how much clearer your head feels. Not to mention, you will be much, *much* more productive in actually getting work tasks completed.

9. Action alleviates anxiety

Anyone who has experienced an anxiety attack, whether they are a diagnosed GAD (generalized anxiety disorder) sufferer or not, can speak to the relationship between control and that crushing, "I cannot breathe" feeling.

The less control you feel you have, the worse the crushing feeling is. You feel like everything is raining down on you and you have no umbrella. You feel like you are standing still while the rest of the world sprints ahead.

Even if you do not know what you need to do to shake this feeling, when you feel it coming on, just do something. Exercise control over something - **anything.** Just make sure you exercise control positively, and not in a way that makes someone else feel inferior.

It does not matter if it feels trivial or silly, just start somewhere. Clean off your desk. Empty your computer's recycling bin. Answer one email. Go on a quick jog or lift some weights.

Eventually, you will make your way to the end of the list. If you leverage this method properly, you will feel better with each small action you take, so that you feel better *before* you get to that last point, not after. Action alleviates anxiety.

10. Stay organized

Disclaimer: This is one of those tips in which I will honestly state, do as I say, not as I do. Now that I have shot my credibility, please proceed.

The make-or-break factor in staying organized is your ability to distinguish between organization as a consistent practice versus an occasional chore. You have probably heard your parents echo this one just a few dozen times, and I heard it even a few more from my Basic Law Enforcement Training school director: If you just put everything back as soon as you are done, you will never lose it.

Moreover, *staying* organized instead of taking a few hours a week to organize will ensure you get more done and feel less stressed. This could not be more relevant for patrol officers. Mentally mark a spot for each piece of equipment and keep it there consistently. You do not want to be searching around for something when the you-know-what hits the fan.

Consistent decluttering offers mental health benefits in addition to the pragmatic value. You should not have to deal with the stress of a cluttered workspace in addition to the dangers/trauma associated with the job. You should not have to go all the way home just to feel decluttered mentally; keeping your areas clean and organized will allow you a much-needed refuge you can return to throughout your shift. Remember: it is all about forming the habit, not the endless messy-clean-messy-clean cycle!

11. Counseling

Where many of the techniques we have covered so far have indirect, albeit powerful, effects on your mental health, counseling is an absolutely crucial head-on approach for officers who experience mental health issues at one time or another. This is the majority of us.

Honestly, counseling should be mandatory for law enforcement officers because, by definition, our career exposes us to things that the brain is not wired to experience. We are subjected to traumatic images and the constant threat of harm - and some officers argue they can just "deal with it"? It is like asking a calculator to spell-check your reports - it is not possible for your brain to deal with this repetitive trauma unless you are a bona fide sociopath.

In *Mental Health Fight of the Heroes in Blue,* I recruited the wisdom of several life coaching, psychology, and neuro-linguistic programming experts who provided some general, yet highly insightful tips about how to deal with the stressors of the job. By seeking counseling for your unique situation, you can access even more personally relevant action plans to keep your mental health at an optimal level.

Seeking counseling is not surrendering or "wussing out." It is simply taking charge of your health and fixing the problem, and it is always confidential. You do not have to be on your last straw. In fact, it is better if you get help when the issues are still nagging and not yet detrimental.

12. Take Breaks

So long as it does not jeopardize your safety, someone else's safety, or an urgent deadline, there is nothing wrong with just walking away for ten minutes. You are not "lazy" or a bad officer because you want to have a few minutes to decompress now and again. Sure, there are some folks in this job and less stressful occupations who abuse break time, but if you genuinely need it to reset yourself mentally, then there is absolutely **no** reason to feel guilty or ashamed.

Your brain functions in waves when it comes to your ability to focus - not a linear/steady trend. Even in low-stress scenarios, if I may be so rude as to bring your attention back to long hours of homework and final exam studying, long periods of sustained work tend to cause serious dips in focus.

In his book *Where There's a Will There's an A,* professor Claude Olney, J.D., discusses this wave-versus-linear function of the brain, concluding that it is best to work in twenty minute intervals with ten minute breaks in between. Yes, this is not realistic for most professions, but the closer you can get to that interval, the better your focus will be.

Mind you, you can take a break from one thing by doing another; you do not necessarily have to stop working completely to be on break.

13. Laugh It Up!

I mean that unsarcastically. Similar to the physiological, mental, and spiritual benefits of smiling is the enigma that is the laugh. Never underestimate the power of laughter - even in the most grim of circumstances.

The "this isn't the time for jokes" mentality, while it might be intended to be respectful or professional, is actually harmful when it comes to your ability to cope with trauma in certain cases. I am not advocating you burst out laughing in the middle of a eulogy commemorating a fallen fellow officer. What I am saying is that you can yuk it up with your brother and sister officers after the service, as you reminisce over the funny things this particular officer did and said.

Laughter heals, it brings people of different traditions together, and it literally fights illness.

Do not believe me? Here is an excerpt straight out of *helpguide.org:*

"Laughter decreases stress hormones and increases immune cells and infection-fighting antibodies, thus improving your resistance to disease. Laughter triggers the release of endorphins, the body's natural feel-good chemicals. Endorphins promote an overall sense of well-being and can even temporarily relieve pain."

This plays into the whole routine of "surrounding yourself with positive (and in this case, funny) people." I will cover that later. In a nutshell, you should seek out people who you can laugh with. You could just watch a set from the uproariously funny *Jim Gaffigan*, of course, but the benefit of laughing in person is that you can build healthy relationships at the same time.

14. Help someone in need

Obviously, it is a rightfully celebrated point of pride among police officers and all who support their efforts that helping people is central to the occupation. One of the greatest ways to add value to your life is to add value to the lives of others, and we are blessed with the opportunity to do that almost every day.

Still, helping others does not have to be work-related. In fact, when you go out of your way when you are off the clock to help someone, even if the deed is very small, you add on an even more genuine layer of altruism that makes it feel even better. Because, after all, you did not have to do that for them.

Offering encouragement to an officer or a distressed person you encounter on a call counts as adding value to someone's life, as does helping a stranger out with a random act of kindness. Add value, feel valuable yourself - that is the simple equation.

This is not to be confused with helping someone out of vanity or selfish intentions. In those cases, as when you are checking something off a list without putting your heart into the deed, you may find that the gratification it gives you is less powerful than you may have hoped.

Of course, apprehending and detaining someone who committed a crime against another person is adding value to be sure, but make an extra effort to help someone when nobody is watching as well. I also challenge you to **not** post your good deed on social media, because that too will diminish the positive impact of it with selfishness.

15. Vent physically on a pillow or punching bag

Giving your pillow a solid thwack or going to town on a punching bag as a means for letting off steam and managing stress does not mean that you are some psycho. Yes, violent criminals often derive joy from simulations of gory violence, but that does not mean the rest of us who are just overworked and overstressed can not vent physically in a healthy way.

Exercise is life-affirming and healthy in so many ways, as we have already covered the feel-good chemicals, stress relief, renewed focus, and so on and so forth. But not all forms of exercise are created equal in the specific types of stress, fatigue, and anger that they address.

I wish I could give you more than anecdotal evidence in this case, but as it happens, there is not a large library of scientific research out there distinguishing between the catharsis level provided from a boxing-style workout versus a more standard cardio/weights regimen.

But boy, does it work for me, as well as several other officers I know. Hitting a bag just feels really, really good when you are stressed, overworked, or frustrated. As long as you are not deriving satisfaction from the thought of hurting someone, it is more than okay. So, go ahead and pound the bag for a while, and do not forget to wrap those wrists! If you are not wearing wraps, then hammer fists or palm heel strikes.

16. Affirmations

And the next stop on our list of "don't worry, you're not crazy if you do this" is the art of talking to yourself in a positive and uplifting way, i.e., affirmations.

It is kind of a funny thought, when you really dive into it, but it really is true that you have a relationship with yourself, and that the way you treat yourself mentally can affect the way you feel about yourself. It is not silly, or pointless, or insane for you to focus on your inner monologue and tweak it for the better.

If you do not examine your self-talk, it will probably just default to the negative thought patterns it has been exposed to, i.e., "retirement can't get here fast enough" or "another day, another problem."

If you recite positive affirmations regularly, however, you will train yourself to not only feel better, but to improve the way you treat yourself and those around you. In the words of the esteemed T. Harv Eker as published in his book, *Secrets of the Millionaire Mind*:

Thoughts lead to feelings. Feelings lead to actions. Actions lead to results.

Conversely, a very wise and short Jedi master once said:

Fear leads to anger. Anger leads to hate. Hate leads to the dark side.

Here are some affirmations you can practice to implant positive thoughts in your head that will lead to positive feelings, actions, and results:

"Today is going to be an outstanding day"
"I am grateful for (name at least three things)"
"I like me"
"I am going to do great things for people"

Over time, you will feel your self-doubt and negativity melt away, and in their place will be a deep well of positive energy.

17. Recall traumatic events in the third person

If you could walk away with just one tip from this book, I would hope it is this one. Especially if you are suffering from PTSD. This is *so* vitally important to overcoming negative responses to trauma and moving on with your life. Here is how it works:

It is unfair to expect someone who has experienced one or more traumatic events to simply not think of those events. The brain will play the trauma again and again as a way of analyzing it and studying it for preventative value - it is just the way it works, unfortunately.

However, you can still take control of the trauma not by attempting to erase it, but by modifying it so that it no longer dominates your thought processes.

Here is how you do it: the next time that dark memory resurfaces, and you begin to feel as if you are actually in that moment again (clammy hands, increased heart rate, etc.), I just want you to focus on one thing - looking at it from the outside. Transition from a first-person perspective to a third-person perspective.

The research and experts largely agree that if you can partially remove yourself from the situation by visualizing the traumatic memory as a kind of "out of body experience," i.e., watching yourself from afar, then you can finally process and overcome it. That is all you have to focus and meditate on when the memory comes back. Third person, not first.

18. Keep your diet on point

I know we have already reviewed a few specific points when it comes to diet and exercise, but I want to revisit this all-important practice from a mental health angle. That is right, dieting is not just for your body. It affects your mood and overall mental health as well.

In an article published on WebMD, Dr. Roxanne Sukol states, "When we eat real food that nourishes us, it becomes the protein-building blocks, enzymes, brain tissue, and neurotransmitters that transfer information and signals between various parts of the brain and body."

In other words, food does not just magically turn into muscle and fat. It also fuels many of the cellular processes involved with registering and interpreting stimuli, emotionally reacting to things, making decisions, and a whole lot more. It directly affects our mental health by literally feeding the processes that govern it.

Given this connection, shoveling junk food down your gullet day in and day out will not keep these vital brain functions running at optimal levels. I am not arguing that a poor diet alone will directly cause anxiety, depression, and PTSD, but it does fertilize the landscape in which these disorders thrive by weakening your mental and emotional faculties across the board.

19. Vent to an extent

"To an extent" being the operative phrase here, because there is a clear threshold between healthy venting and going off on an unhealthy rant that just makes your anger and frustration feel even worse.

You should never bottle in the anger, disappointment, and sadness you feel, because when these fester in your mind, they contribute to mental health disorders like depression, anxiety, and others. Hence, venting is actually a healthy practice, but only if you give yourself constraints. Talk it out with a friend, but for both their sake and yours, put a predetermined time limit on it. Once you get past a point, you will just start looping, and each pass you make through the things that frustrate you, will feel more intense.

Establishing this healthy framework is step one of two. Step number two is vitally important - work with your friend to create actionable steps toward a resolution. If you just vent without working towards a resolution, then you might as well tell your poor buddy to meet you at the same bar tomorrow and the next day, because that is where you will be. Make sense?

Vent, come up with an action plan, execute, and hopefully feel marginally better. It is not magic, and it will take time, but it is better than just venting.

20. Read

How exotic, right? I realize this is a non-starter for a lot of people, but hear me out for just a moment. You know that anxious/overwhelmed feeling you get when you are reminded of the fact that you should read because it is good for you, but you do not have the time? Well, not to get too personal, but let us take a look at your time, shall we?

Mindlessly scrolling through Facebook after work? Swap it out and read. Kicking back with that new Netflix hit? Keep it to two episodes or less and then read. Point being, reading is one of the most productive pastimes that is still really entertaining once you find the right book, so it is a win-win if you just swap out your less productive pastimes with it.

Simply sitting down and reading will help immensely with stress and anxiety. To add an extra layer of mental health support on, you can read positive and uplifting books that give you a new perspective on life. It does not have to be some modern self-help book for police officers, either. You can read Seneca, for goodness sakes, the ancient Roman stoic philosopher, and learn plenty about what it means to be happy in the darkest of times.

21. Sleep

Just like dieting, sleep is one of those items that transcends physical health benefits, bearing great significance in the realm of mental health as well.

Even a little kid eventually learns that a lack of sleep will cause you to feel cranky and easily frustrated by things that would not normally affect you. As it turns out, a healthy sleep schedule is also vital in alleviating or completely deterring more permanent mental health conditions.

If you are experiencing sleep difficulties and you can not pin down a physical cause, it may be an indicator that there is an underlying mental health issue in play, as with depression or PTSD especially. Even if you do not feel sad or anxious or traumatized all day, it does not mean these elements are not present in your subconscious.

Some law enforcement officers, again referencing that "tough guy or girl" socialization we have to deal with, tell themselves that they can just tough it out for 24-48 hours with no issue. They think that caffeine alone will get the job done, but this could not be farther from the truth. Not only is your judgment and emotional state impaired when sleep-deprived, you could even *hallucinate*. Sounds just a tiny bit troublesome for, I do not know, a law enforcement officer!

Seven to eight hours, friends. Seven to eight!

22. Limit your caffeine

I realize I just uttered pure blasphemy, but if I have to become the bad guy just to keep you safe and healthy, then so be it. Yes, I realize coffee is cop gold, but even too much gold is a bad thing. Right?

According to a study by Villanova University, 90% of Americans consume caffeine in one form or another. Caffeine, as you know, is a stimulant. Our jobs, as you also know, are also stimulants in themselves. One second, you are bored to tears, and the next, you are in a life-or-death situation.

Add a few shots of caffeine into the mix, and you have yourself a seriously overworked mind.

Coffee impairs your ability to access magnesium, which is normally used to combat anxiety among other things. Caffeine is also a vasoconstrictor, meaning it tightens your blood vessels up, reducing blood flow to your brain. You do not have to be a neurologist to know that is not helpful at all in the law enforcement scenario.

I may sound harsh, but look, I do not mean to go straight-laced on you. If you enjoy making that wholesome morning cup of coffee to get a little pep in your step, I totally get it. I get the best coffee there is from *Monki Beanz.*

Remember though, sucking on multiple cups a day and/or energy drinks is not going to do anything for your physical *or* mental health. To be frank, energy drinks are awful for you. I know, I know, how could I state such a thing?!

23. Deep breathing

Starting to catch onto the theme here? The mind and body are connected by many anchors, and deep breathing is definitely one of them. When it comes to mental health, taking a deep breath (or seventeen) is a great way to get your mind to say, "Phew, thanks. I needed that." This is because deep breathing is associated in your brain with the rest-and-digest side of things, not the fight-or-flight impulse.

Even if things go well on a call, we as law enforcement officers have to go through stress to reach that resolution. This is when deep breathing comes into play.

According to a *Harvard Medical School* article, when you take shorter breaths, you are training the brain to feel anxious. This makes sense, because when a bear pops out of the clearing five feet in front of you on that hunting trip, how do you think your breathing will be?

Of course, there is no way to completely avoid stressors, but deep breathing is an exemplary way to cope with said stressors so they take a much smaller toll, allowing you the longevity to make it through a shift without feeling completely wrecked.

Remember: breathe slowly through your nose, allow the stomach (not chest) to expand, and slowly let it out as you contract the abdomen. Nice, deep, and slow, not shallow.

24. Moderate the alcohol

Just because you are not an alcoholic, does not mean that drinking is not a harmful crutch if you do not watch it closely. I will be the last one to wag my finger at you and lecture that you should not drink at all. For goodness sakes, if anyone deserves a drink, it is you and me! Cheers! Moderation, however, is paramount.

If you find yourself craving alcohol because you *need* it to relax or feel happy, then we are teetering on the brink of alcoholism. Even if you do not binge drink a case every other night, this kind of attachment is a telltale sign. Obviously, drinking to excess will not only act as a crutch in terms of mental health, but it will have harmful effects on your physical health. The gut is just the beginning.

As I pointed out in *Mental Health Fight of the Heroes in Blue,* alcoholism is romanticized by our culture to an extent, which unfortunately gives people a kind of halfway incentive to go down that path, or at least does not discourage them as much as it should. After all, what do many of us do after a shift, especially on Thursday or Friday? Happy hour!

However, steady over-consumption of alcohol can affect what we United States Marines call the "brain housing group." In all seriousness, the more you drink the more your serotonin levels are reduced, which rolls out the red carpet for depression and anxiety.

25. Dark chocolate cake! You heard me

I thought that after all the harping I have done in this chapter, I would at least give you something to feel hopeful about. Of course, my opening disclaimer in this case is that refined sugar is never a good thing and you should stay away, *however,* it really is true that dark chocolate can help your mental acuity in a number of ways.

Per a *Mental Health America* article, "The flavonoids, caffeine, and theobromine in chocolate are thought to work together to improve alertness and mental skills."

So, on the one hand, sugar is not so great for a number of your mental faculties. However, on the other hand, dark chocolate is actually helpful. There are two scenarios in which I believe you could make this work to your advantage:

1. Let dark chocolate cake be your one treat that you seldom have while maintaining a very low sugar diet otherwise, exercising, meditating, etc…

2. Skip the cake part and just find some pure dark chocolate that has way less sugar. This is only for people who enjoy the *actual* taste of dark chocolate. If that is you, this is a win-win!

*****

I will never forget earning that nice shiny police badge twenty-six years ago. It was a proud day and the badge was complimented with fresh new uniforms and clean polished boots. In my mind, I knew who I was and nothing was going to halt me from stopping crime. I was going to be that tough line of defense for the good, protecting them from those that intend to do harm. This is the mentality I was taught in the police academy. I just wish they would have taught us more about what ended up being more of my story working as a police officer.

The academy instructors never taught us about how to prepare for the draining twelve-hour work days/nights, the physical and mental toll of rotating shifts, the effects on a family from working weekends and holidays, and how to cope with the trauma we would be exposed to on a consistent basis. I could go on and on, but what I remember the most was that we were just molded to be superheroes. Police are primarily trained to run toward the danger while others are scrambling to escape.

The narrative of training is really no different transitioning from an academy to a police department or sheriff's office. You are rightfully expected to respond to a call, no matter how much of a dangerous threat it poses. There are policies and procedures to follow on every call. Unfortunately, the policies and procedures at most departments do not even touch on the aftermath of an officer's mind and body from unswerving exposure to threats and shock. This is not the case with all departments, but at some, the officers might be provided access to a gym or maybe cheaper memberships at local health clubs.

In my career I have spent all of my time in the patrol division. I have worked in a small department and am currently working in a mid-size department. I have worked in New Jersey and North Carolina. My title is currently Patrol Lieutenant.

When I was a cop in New Jersey, shifts were twelve hours. A vast number of agencies across the country do twelve-hour shifts. The challenge with my department in New Jersey was the formidable schedule of rotating every shift from days to nights. For example, I would work two days, then I was off for two days. When I would return to work, I had to work three nights in a row, take two days off, and then back on day shift. To add to the daunting task, was the fact I lived sixty-three miles away! In those thirteen years I had a family but could not afford anything closer that fit our needs. It was a weight of stress. Who needs sleep and recovery right?

I lived on three big cups of coffee and at least two donuts (to meet the requirements of the stereotype) to complete that sugar high of surviving twelve hours. Low quality "food" and too much caffeine, shift after shift. Who am I to complain?! I was just a cop doing what so many other cops did just to try to stay awake! Mission first! Health and wellness second! So I thought. Oh, and did I mention that I put on 35,000 miles a year on my personal car?

During those tasking years I had a few car crashes throughout my three hour round trip back and forth from home to work, then back home. One morning while driving home at 6:00 am feeling the fatigue of the shift I had just completed; I fell asleep behind the wheel. I was woken up from my hazardous slumber by the glaring sound of a New Jersey State Patrol siren. I was driving right at the Trooper! I am lucky to have survived that dangerous moment. It scared me, a lot. But, I was trained to be a superhero right?

Do you know what it is really the most shocking aspect during those thirteen years? The sad but true answer is that I never thought of my family. I, like so many other officers, thought only about the job and what I was trained to do. I am a superhero is what I thought. That all dynamically changed in 2001.

In 2001, the horrendous diet, long hours, and stress took a toll on my health. I was diagnosed with Gastro Reflux Esophageal Disease and my gallbladder had collapsed. The gallbladder needed to be removed, and the doctor prescribed me medicine. The doctor also firmly instructed me to get more sleep, and altar my diet for the better. I was on it! For a few weeks, I was healthy as could be, but then bad habits returned. I was eating complete garbage again and not getting sleep. I thought I could do it. Why did I stop? Because I am a superhuman right? I do not experience stress and challenges like mortal humans. What I failed to realize is that I was destroying my mind and body. Let us not forget as well that my family was an afterthought, and therefore my marriage started to become strained.

A few years later my wife and I decided to move to North Carolina with our kids. I started as a patrol officer and was surely not making the money I was making on the job up north. I was working off-duty assignments to feed my family. Two years after I started, I was promoted to sergeant and then eventually earned lieutenant. The transition from officer to a supervisor's position put a different stress on me. My concern was not doubting my ability to do the job, but I had officers I was responsible for and wanted to lead them to my upmost desire and aptitude. I felt stressed because I cared that they stayed safe and were treated right. The retired veterans I learned from taught me a lot about leadership, but it was stressful. I originally never ever wanted to be in a supervisor role, but other officers encouraged me to do it, so I did. That is another challenge about the job of a police officer, balancing out being there for your fellow officers, and your family.

I did my best to remain the finest leader I could be, but it started to take a toll on my physical and mental well-being. Can you guess why? It is because we police officers cannot just switch psychological gears from work to home. The risks of the job, thinking about my subordinates, and trying to make sure I handled calls well, would sit on my mind. I began undergoing a waterfall of negative effects such as lack of sleep, headaches, horrible eating, stomach aches, consistent sickness, and mood swings. In a way I was working twenty-four hours a day. Did I mention I was still on a rotating shift? It was every twenty-eight days rather than every time I would return to work, but still, rotating. With all of it, came results.

I started to develop additional problems as I aged. But once again, I was the superhero and work came first. Seeing a pattern here? Ok, back on track. You see, I had to make management happy but I wanted my officers to be better off. Once again, I put off personal matters, and my marriage started to strain again. Unfortunately, this occurs way too frequently in law enforcement. Due to the added stress of the trauma on the job, and stress of management, it had its results.

I will never forget my lovely champion of a wife told me that our marriage was failing and that my kids were suffering too. I was never taught in the police academy about how to manage a family while being in law enforcement. It hit me like a left hook, as it does so many other officers. In July of 2019, I went to my doctor because I started to develop anxiety. The doctor gave me a prescription but said, "Kevin, you **need** *to change your life." I took action, and started to go to a therapist. I will never forget the therapist telling me that law enforcement was killing me and becoming toxic. It hit me so hard, because I knew that she was undoubtedly correct. I stopped doing off-duty and I turned my phone off when I was not working. I started coaching my son's baseball team and tied to go to the gym on a routine basis. For the first time, in a long time, I started to feel great and the pieces of life were being put back into place. Then the unthinkable happened.*

On October 4, 2019 I was diagnosed with rectal cancer. The totality of the stress, bad diet, lack of sleep, anxiety, and family problems all came to a head. I lost the battle of thinking I was a superhero who could stop crime without having to take care of myself. I praise God above that I was diagnosed when I was, I mean, since I had it of course. The doctor told me if the cancer was not discovered, I would have not lived past age fifty, and I am currently forty-nine. I am still fighting the cancer and it will not defeat me like the stress of law enforcement.

No police officer thinks they will ever have mental and physical health issues, or marital issues, parenting issues, or even worse, commit suicide. These are dark realities of the job and it is up to you to act with healthy habits and gain a strong positive perspective. You can do this.

I would like to thank Scott for letting me write this because I would have bought this book twenty-five years ago. Scott has a ton of high-quality advice he has a wealth of knowledge because he himself has gone through the trauma and stress just like I have. I can tell you his main goal with this book is to keep at least one officer thinking the right way when you enter this profession. Notice I stated the profession and not your life. Keep a balance between the two. I would also like to advise you that when your supervisor hands you that first citation book keep this book next to it. Your life is more important that a traffic ticket. I wish you the best of luck in this career and remember you are the only one that can keep you healthy.

-Lieutenant Kevin Tatur

Chapter 3
Supporting Your Spiritual Well-Being

Law enforcement or not, faith plays many fundamental roles for those who choose to embrace it, including overcoming adversity, being patient with others, resisting temptation, choosing wholesome and productive choices, and much more.

Let me first disclaim that I do not pretend to speak from a position of righteousness. Just like you, I have made a mistake or 415. But that is all the more reason for me to seek God's wisdom, favor, and love. Like you, I am a sinner who is loved by God. I believe in one universal church (aka Catholic), and I reject Satan and all his evil ways.

Speaking of, Satan has a number of especially sneaky avenues he uses to tempt police officers in particular, because after all, you are a fallible human being like the rest of us. Through strong faith, however, you will be that much more fortified against temptation. You will be empowered to direct your intentions whole-heartedly toward works of good, on the clock or off. Without faith, your life and career can really go off the rails - who wants that?

If you are an atheist/agnostic or if you follow a completely different belief system, I completely understand if you want to skip this chapter. Either way, I support your journey towards a healthier and happier law enforcement career just as much.

There is still plenty of generally helpful wisdom(i.e., not trying to convert you or rattle off pages of scripture in a row) in this section for you to benefit from, but if you are not comfortable, I will see you in the next chapter.

I pray my actions and words will shine the light of God, which is faith, hope, and love to God's will and fellow man.

1. Energy is absolutely a thing!

In the Western world especially, we are still fairly ignorant to the concept of energy as it concerns relationships, interactions, and work. Let me phrase it this way: You know that tired, cranky feeling you get after having a conversation with a negative person? In many cases, and this is the worst part, you not only feel tired out by their morose perspective, but infected by it as well.

You do not have to be some crystal-ball reading magic man or woman to at least appreciate the concept of energy on this basic level. Unfortunately, this example (of the negative person) does not just go away five minutes later - with enough exposure, you will become a negative person as well.

Even if you are not the most "religious" (pun intended) scholar, at least making an effort to surround yourself with the positive message of the Bible, can be very powerful in offsetting this negative energy. We Christians believe that God's holy spirit was left to us in order to guide us in towards God's teachings. These teachings include making better decisions and maintaining a perspective of gratitude. The more you learn and the closer you get to God, the better you will feel.

2. Read the Bible

I mean, it is not like you did not see this one coming, right? I cannot recommend this enough. Do not make it this huge undertaking in your mind. Do not stress it. Do not build it up. Simply block out a little time each day, get comfortable, and read your Bible. This is sage advice from the likes of Police Chaplain Lonnie Clouse of *First Responders 1st* - just read the thing.

"Yeah yeah, I know Scott. I have heard it a thousand times."

Here is the thing: It is different in your situation. The Bible helps all of us overcome challenges and make better decisions in unique ways, but in the case of a law enforcement officer, the healing word simply could not be more essential.

Chaplain Clouse gave me solid advice. He said to think about being a parent, which is a reality for me and many others. You would want your kids to communicate with you whenever they feel scared, angry, sad, or whatever, right? That is the same way God feels, and by talking with him, you will receive water for your parched soul and the strength to carry on.

As much as I appreciate podcasts (especially the free ones), no single nugget of wisdom I have learned from them can shine a candle to the word of God. If it feels like the book was made for you, that is because it was.

3. Psalm 91 before every shift

The psalms of the Bible are a great place to look for advice, comfort, perspective, and more. Psalm 91 is no exception, and I would like to call attention to it so that you can benefit from it as I have.

[1] Whoever dwells in the shelter of the Most High
   will rest in the shadow of the Almighty.[a]
[2] I will say of the Lord, "He is my refuge and my fortress,
   my God, in whom I trust."
[3] Surely he will save you
   from the fowler's snare
   and from the deadly pestilence.
[4] He will cover you with his feathers,
   and under his wings you will find refuge;
   his faithfulness will be your shield and rampart.
[5] You will not fear the terror of night,
   nor the arrow that flies by day,
[6] nor the pestilence that stalks in the darkness,
   nor the plague that destroys at midday.
[7] A thousand may fall at your side,
   ten thousand at your right hand,
   but it will not come near you.
[8] You will only observe with your eyes
   and see the punishment of the wicked.
[9] If you say, "The Lord is my refuge,"
   and you make the Most High your dwelling,
[10] no harm will overtake you,
   no disaster will come near your tent.
[11] For he will command his angels concerning you
   to guard you in all your ways;
[12] they will lift you up in their hands,
   so that you will not strike your foot against a stone.
[13] You will tread on the lion and the cobra;
   you will trample the great lion and the serpent.
[14] "Because he[b] loves me," says the Lord, "I will rescue him;
   I will protect him, for he acknowledges my name.
[15] He will call on me, and I will answer him;
   I will be with him in trouble,

> *I will deliver him and honor him.*
> *[16] With long life I will satisfy him*
>   *and show him my salvation."*

God is here to protect you, and all you have to do is call on him, trust him, and get to know him. Recite this before every shift not just to protect yourself, but to face those around you with a calmer and more positive demeanor.

I would also like to offer up the police officer's prayer, contributed anonymously, so you can have something that speaks even more directly to your experience:

Oh Almighty God,
Whose Great Power and Eternal Wisdom Embraces the Universe,
Watch Over All Policemen and Law Enforcement Officers.
Protect Them from Harm in the Performance of Their Duty to Stop Crime, Robberies, Riots, and Violence.
We Pray,
Help Them Keep Our Streets and Homes Safe Day and Night.
We Recommend Them to Your Loving Care Because Their Duty is Dangerous.
Grant Them Your Unending Strength and Courage in Their Daily Assignments.
Dear God,
Protect These Brave Men and Women,
Grant Them Your Almighty Protection,
Unite Them Safely with Their Families After Duty Has Ended.
Amen.

4. Prayer for the intercession of St. Michael

Regardless of what is happening overseas, police wake up every day and report to an unending war. Until God closes the curtain (and raises it anew), there will be no end to the crime, the suffering, and the hate that police officers encounter on a regular basis.

On the one hand, police are up against the very urgent and obvious threat of physical harm, while on the other, they are also subjected to increased temptations.

That is why I want to call attention to this particular prayer. The prayer for the intercession of St. Michael is not just asking for intercession to help us win a war against men. It is also about rebuking the *evil* that exists in those men - evil that threatens to tempt us as Christians.

The way I see it, this prayer is not just about keeping you safe, helping you subdue the bad guys without being harmed, and stopping crime. This prayer is also about keeping your own faults and your own temptation in check, and asking for the intercession of St. Michael. No, you are not directly worshipping him, you are asking him. Here it is:

"Saint Michael the Archangel, defend us in battle. Be our protection against the wickedness and snares of the devil; May God rebuke him, we humbly pray; And do thou, O Prince of the Heavenly Host, by the power of God, thrust into hell Satan and all evil spirits who prowl about the world, seeking the ruin of souls." -Amen.

5. Philippians 4:6-7

I do not believe it is sacrilegious to say that, upon first encountering these verses, a police officer can be a little frustrated. "Do not worry," really?

But give it a second to ruminate. Think about *why* you do not have to worry. If it were because something as superficial as, "Because if you make it out of this shift alive, you can go to happy hour," then you are darn right there is still a reason to worry.

There is just one thing in this entire universe powerful enough to calm your spirit and erase your worry in the face of danger: the protection of God. *That is* why you do not have to worry. When we surrender to Him, He takes much better care of us than we ever could ourselves.

That is what Philippians 4:6-7 means to me, and even if it does not hit you the exact same way, I hope you find even greater relief in its wise words.

⁶ Don not worry about anything, but pray about everything. With thankful hearts offer up your prayers and requests to God.⁷ Then, because you belong to Christ Jesus, God will bless you with peace that no one can completely understand. And this peace will control the way you think and feel."

6.   Isaiah 54:17

Generally, church-going folks tend to go about their affairs with an air of humility, but that is not all God was about. Being kind, humble, and patient is no doubt essential to walking the straight and narrow, but there are also many situations in which you must say no. You must close your doors and offer rebuke to wickedness, whether in physical confrontations or otherwise.

To me, this verse is a reminder not only of the protection of God, but of our role in rebuking evil. He even goes so far as to say that we can be vindicated as we are refuting people who accuse us.

On the surface, that does not sound very "sunshine and rainbow-y," but not everything about being a Christian is. Without further ado, here is Isaiah 54:17

> 17 No weapon forged against you will prevail,
>   and you will refute every tongue that accuses you.
> This is the heritage of the servants of the Lord,
>   and this is their vindication from me,"
> declares the Lord.

See what I mean? It is not about being a snobby elitist or a jerk because you are in God's corner. It is about aligning yourself with the truth and refusing to be tainted by the greatest liar who ever lived.

7. Isaiah 41:10-12

We visit Isaiah again, this time to learn just how far God will go to protect his believers.

Isaiah 41:10-12 states:

> So do not fear, for I am with you;
> do not be dismayed, for I am your God.
> I will strengthen you and help you;
>   I will uphold you with my righteous right hand.
>
> 11 "All who rage against you
>   will surely be ashamed and disgraced;
> those who oppose you
>   will be as nothing and perish.
> 12 Though you search for your enemies,
>   you will not find them.
> Those who wage war against you
>   will be as nothing at all.

I want to make very clear that the point here is not to relish in your enemies' defeat. The point is to trust in the awesome power and righteousness of God. He loves you so much, he is willing to destroy anyone who threatens to harm you. By believing in Him, you are not just making yourself feel better or trying to suck up. You are arming yourself with protection from evil.

8. Download the YouVersion App

We as Christians need to hang onto every possible opportunity we have to make the word of God more accessible. We have all heard the excuses. I do not have time to read the Bible, I am tired, it is too big to take with me to work (or wherever else), I lost it, etc.

You know, it is not a coincidence that it is getting harder in this modern world to connect with the word. We are not just victims of coincidence - we are being actively targeted by Satan, who wants to distract us from the Bible. I am not saying technology and modern conveniences are evil, but they can *sometimes* be used for that purpose.

Point being, if we could make it just as easy to access the bible as it is to check our social media, then there is no more excuse. I am guilty as charged. Chaplain Lonnie, mentioned above, tends to agree. That is why the *YouVersion App* is so important: it meets you where you are.

In addition, you can customize your reading experience to guide you through some of the struggles or temptations you may be facing, like anxiety, courage, depression, success, and a whole lot more.

All of this is for free. That is right, I said this app is absolutely free! Hallelujah!!

9. Spiritual Music

As with so many other access points throughout the Christian faith, we have to break through a solid wall of stereotypes in this case especially.

Look, not all Christian music is cheesy or boring or super old. There are plenty of mainstream, popular bands who have charted some of the greatest hits in history that celebrated God in their music.

It is not that cheesy and boring Christian music is at all diminished in its value or its importance to God and all of us, but you should not have to cringe your way through music you do not like just to get the message.

For example, I like Toby Mac, Skillet, Lecrae, and Switchfoot to name a few. Google them. We are so blessed to have great musicians like this who are driven to work the word of God into their music AND do so with tremendous talent. It is an awesome way to keep you feeling positive, grateful, and peaceful no matter what you are going through on any given day.

Not sure where to get started? Just take five minutes on YouTube with the above bands. I covered a few genres there, so you should be able to find something you like without too much digging (that autoplay can take you to some weird places, right?)

Peaceful without putting you to sleep, intense without objectifying people and glorifying violence, drugs, and immoral sex. Win-win!!

10. Daily Devotional

This is a great opportunity for you to express your love of God, or to get to know him better, or to further your relationship in whichever manner you are most comfortable doing. When done right, a daily devotional is something that speaks directly to your life experience and your passions.

For example, if you love to draw, sing, write, or practice any other art form, you can dedicate a piece of your artwork to God every day as a way of staying consistent with your faith.

If you like being a police officer (wink wink), then glorify him after you safely complete a traffic stop. Praise his name when you stop a violent person from hurting someone.

That being said, I do want to encourage you to learn something new with each experience. Look up some more verses and incorporate them into your expression. It feels good to practice what you are good at, but any accomplished person will tell you that it is all about practicing what you are less familiar with, growing, and changing.

Just because this is a personal experience, by the way, does not mean you have to do it all alone. Fortunately, there are a plethora of resources out there you can use to give you inspiration for your daily devotional if you are not sure how to get started or what to do next. It is one of the best habits in existence, devoting your time and a piece of yourself to the One who has devoted so much love to you.

11. Jeremiah 29:11

It may sound like a cryptic, half-finished thought on the first read, but there is *so* much value in understanding the idea introduced in Jeremiah 29:11. This verse helps to answer many of the questions we dare to critique God with in our short-sighted moments of weakness.

Before I explain further, let us just roll out Jeremiah 29:11:

"For I know the plans I have for you," declares the LORD, "plans to prosper you and not to harm you, plans to give you hope and a future."

Here is what I have learned from this verse: even if it seems like God is not listening, or even working against you, you are only capturing a tiny dip in an otherwise upward trend. We only have a tiny picture of our existence to work with, but God can see the whole thing, and he is making sure it ends up in a good place for those who believe in Him.

So, when people ask why God lets terrible atrocities happen to innocent people, it comforts me to know that he has an individual plan for each of us, and that the plan is to help us prosper in the end. Though we may indeed endure suffering on this planet, our mysterious God is making sure that no negative situation ever ends up the way it looks for his believers.

I like to think that the ever-faithful and patient Job would have read this and smiled, because it is snippets of wisdom such as these that help us impatient and short-sighted humans get a sneak peak at God's long game.

12. Attend church! Be active in the spiritual community!

Fellowship is such an integral part of faith, it is crazy. God wants us not only to believe in Him, but to share those beliefs among fellow sinners and to support each other so we can follow His ways like the big family that we are.

Think about it this way - did you ever do any sports or clubs in high school or college? A year or two after quitting that sport, did you find it hard to train again without teammates to play/compete with and a coach hollering at you? That is kind of how I view fellowship.

Of course, being a part of the spiritual community is not about competing with one another or screaming at each other to do this and do that. It is about lovingly supporting each other so that we may all follow that righteous path to the best of our ability.

Also, as a law enforcement officer or otherwise, going to church and talking with people in the spiritual community is a great way to relieve stress, vent (for a set period of time, remember?), find support, and support others. The need to escape stress is a very easy path towards drugs and abusive behaviors, but thankfully, God has them all beat by a landslide in terms of lasting comfort and happiness.

13. Chaplain or Peer Support Program

Why the heck one or both of these are not currently present at every police department, sheriff's office, and law enforcement agency nationwide is beyond me. I would never propose that we force mandatory participation or anything like that, but this resource would be absolutely invaluable for police officers, especially since it would meet them literally right where they are.

I am not ashamed at all to admit that I have consulted the Chaplain a time or two when struggling with various issues throughout my career, and in many instances, the Chaplain provided more helpful advice than the counselors did. It is not to knock their job, of course, but there is more to mental health than just mental health. If you ignore the spiritual element, you will only be able to dig so deep.

The following points will take on more of a rapid-fire format for a few reasons. First, they are quotes, so they are naturally shorter. Secondly, I do not want to sully the impact these pieces of wisdom may have on you by clouding your interpretation with (more of) my interpretation. Finally, by keeping these nice and short, I can make it easy for you to look them up and repeat them in your daily insanity-fighting mantras.

14. **"Don't measure the size of the mountain; talk to the One who can move it."**
    -Max Lucado

15. **"Courage is fear that has said its prayers and decided to go forward anyway."**
    -Joyce Meyer

16. **"If all Jesus ever knew about you is what you told Him in prayer, how well would he know you?**
    -Father Mike Schmitz

17. **"Be the type of person that when your feet touch the floor in the morning the devil says, 'Oh crap...they're up!"**
    -Dwayne Johnson

18. **"God uses no one until He first puts them through the storm. The greater your mission, the greater your storm."**
    -Pastor John Hagee

19. **"Focusing on the negative only makes a difficult journey more difficult."**
    -TobyMac

20. **"Courage is grace under pressure."**
    -Ernest Hemingway

21. **"Have courage for the great sorrows of life and patience for the small ones; and when you have**

laboriously accomplished your daily task, go to sleep in peace. God is awake."
-Victor Hugo

22. Name the blessings

This technique comes straight from an article by Victor Parachin at *Vibrant Life*. If I may be a little extra insistent on this particular point, let me just holler one time: DO THIS! It is so vitally important that you keep a running dialogue of the things you are grateful for, and just like everything else, if you do not put it to a schedule, this great habit will fall by the wayside without you even realizing it.

Here is what Parachin had to say on the topic of naming your blessings:

Too often we go through life oblivious to the good that comes flowing into our lives. Try this spiritual exercise for one week: At the end of the first day, identify a blessing that came to you from a family member. At the end of the second day, a blessing from a neighbor. Third day, from a friend. Fourth day, from a work colleague. Fifth day, from a stranger. Sixth day, from a child. On the seventh day, a blessing that came from an "enemy."

The point here is multi-faceted. First, maintaining a grateful mindset is imperative for law enforcement officers especially, because it helps to fight negative thought processes. Obviously, reflecting on blessings you have received will help you to keep this effort alive. Secondly, it teaches us that blessings are not always wrapped with a bow. Sometimes, even something you thought was a slight against you turns out to be a blessing.

23. Meditation

Well fancy that, we see meditation popping up yet again. Let us see here...that makes mind, body, and now spirit. Getting the picture here? Meditation is all-encompassing in its benefits. In addition to balancing you out mentally and physically, it keeps you more centered in your spiritual life as well.

Now more than ever, meditation is critical for cutting through the technology-induced fog that has shrouded our extremely busy daily routines. Go ahead and tell yourself that it is only for sandal-wearing, patchouli-covered wussies. Go ahead and tell yourself that they are the loonies. Even if you were to voice such an opinion, it would just roll right off, because that is a big part of what meditation does.

You will feel peaceful and calm, but not in a sedative way - you will still be able to meet a high energy demand when it presents itself, whether this occurs in the physical, mental, or spiritual domain. **That is the true power of balance**.

By calming your mind, meditation helps to clear the way for your running dialogue with God and with yourself. It will not do everything for you, but meditation is especially great at getting all those distractions and excuses out of the way.

24. Release your hatred and/or bitterness

The clinging power of negativity is a bane to all who would strive for a successful career, family life, or anything else for that matter. No matter what a person does to you, you have to eventually let it go.

I understand. You are a human being. And we parents can attest to how we feel about anyone who has ever messed with our kids.

Whether it is a bad romantic relationship, a coworker saying or doing something, or someone who just rubs you the wrong way on a call, it can be really, really hard to let go of certain offenses, especially if they are personal and very harmful in nature.

Still, even though it may seem unfair, the more resentment you hold on to, merited or not, the more your spiritual health suffers. Hate is a bottomless pit. If you just jump in, you will never hit the bottom and move on, so make sure to control it.

This is not to say that it is your lot in life as a Christian to be a pushover. Obviously, it is your right to protect yourself and the ones you love, and it is equally justifiable that you rebuke someone who has wronged you in a productive manner. The point I am really honing in on right now is that *after* the event, you have to let it go, lest your spiritual well-being be compromised.

25. Matthew 5:9

It hits me right in the feels every single time. I have saved one of my absolute favorite verses for last:

"Blessed are the peacemakers, for they will be called children of God."

Does that not just light you up? As a law enforcement officer, I felt like this verse spoke directly to me (and you), and honestly, it does. *God cares about us.* Like, "us," as in, police.

It is not only a motivational, feel-good kind of verse to read, but it also serves as a reminder. It is no secret that the past decade especially has been challenging in terms of the public perception of police. Our every move is being monitored like never before, thanks to social media, body cams, and smartphones, and even though it is great for accountability, this actually compounds the very issue that leads to misconduct: stress.

I am not interested in fanning the flames when it comes to debating the justifiability of officer-involved shooting x or y, but the bottom line is this: We must never forget why God put us here as police officers. He believes in us. He knows we chose to be tough enough to handle it. He knows we can provide peace to people who are hurt, distressed, confused, and depressed. He knows we can protect people with our lives.

As someone who takes pride in this verse and spreads that energy all through the department and beyond, you can be the example that other officers follow.

*****

It would be so easy to call him a monster. To look at the slow destruction of our marriage and increasingly problematic behavior and erase all thoughts of good and decency in him. I could hold onto the night that I woke to him turning on the light of my bedroom at 1:45 in the morning, harassing me about the guy I was seeing. I quietly begged him to go outside to be stopped by my mother on the stairs. I told her it would be fine that I would talk to him and be right back in. I never feared him physically hurting me. I had no concern other than irritation. What happened in those next 10 minutes changed our lives forever.

My truth is that we are never just one thing. We aren't even the sum of our parts; we are the gray areas. He was a man that grew up in a difficult situation who tried to escape by joining the Marine Corps. In that institution he found a purpose and another family. Those connections are the fabric that makes units strong. They don't prepare you to lose those family members or the additional stressors of your job. This impacted him on dual fronts in his time in the USMC and in law enforcement.

We met in Iraq, what I affectionately called Spring Break 2005.He was an Explosive Ordnance Disposal (EOD) Tech. They were the rock stars of Marines, and even I wasn't immune. There is something primal about a man who has the balls to disarm an IED, and he looked like G.I. Joe Ken. With the status also came the very real consequences of the job. EOD techs died at a higher rate because, explosives, and they were targeted by the insurgents. Countless times during the deployment I heard that someone "got whacked." This was their description of the death of one of their brothers. It was how they compartmentalized to move forward.

With his second deployment to Iraq a few months after we returned, I excused certain behaviors. I started molding myself to manage his moods. He was jealous and unreasonable with his expectations. I attributed it to being away from home and stress. I assumed it would get better when he returned, I was committed to him by our relationship and our bonds as Marines.

After returning home, he made the decision to get out of the USMC and join the police department. He thought this would give him a similar bond and structure as the military while allowing the freedom of a "civilian life."

Initially he enjoyed the change, people responded to his innate leadership ability and charm. He was even class president when he went through the academy. He chose to work in the most violent area of the city. He told Scott that he "would do it for free it was so fun." He was quickly exposed to children living in bad conditions, gruesome homicides, encounters with suspects possessing assault rifles, and so much more. But when the new hype and excitement wore off and things started to slow down, reality started to catch up to him. His mind had not been trained to handle balancing "normal" life with being a police officer and the aftermath of war.

The risky nature of his job, pulling ten-hour shifts, looking for people doing something wrong, and experiencing emotional roller coasters were starting to distress him in every area of his life. He became exceedingly suspicious of everyone. He assumed the perspective that everyone was guilty of something, including me, his wife. Any flaw in a response, any name that came up too often is a lead to be investigated - a warranted interrogation. Unfortunately, he also started to think the rules did not apply to him, and there were more negative changes in his behavior patterns as a result. The hypervigilance he practiced during war and patrol was becoming an impairment. All I wanted was the doting man with healthy respect for the rules to reappear.

The behaviors got worse the longer he was an officer. He acted like he was the judge and jury for everyone's life - especially mine. He treated me as though I was naive of every man's intentions, and it was up to him to dictate my actions in response to male attention. This was especially glaring when I had Reserve duty. He made my mandatory weekends unbearable, and the first Annual Training after our marriage was hell. I spent hours in my barracks room arguing with him about who sat where at chow and every conversation I had.

The problems continued to escalate, and we separated in 2008. During this time he would badger me about my whereabouts, harass my friends, actively intimidate people he didn't want in my life. I wasn't afraid of him hurting me because he was never physically abusive; he didn't scream at me; he would embarrass and harass me calling me 20-30 times a day inquiring what I was doing and who I was with; but knew he would ever put his hands on me.

Eventually we decided to try to make our marriage work. I hoped that recommitting and contorting to his views would give us both peace. From the outside most people thought that we were the perfect couple. Countless times people would say how much they wanted to be like us. To be fair, when we were among friends and he felt in control of the situation, things were great. It was any time he wasn't able to be the alpha in the room he had an issue, and that hypervigilance would exert itself in full force. Throughout our relationship it manifested when I was at school, work, or reserve duty and a man's name came up to many times. Being in the USMC and working on a trading desk, my bosses and counterparts were predominantly male.

It became clear to me that things were not going to work with us, but I knew well that he wouldn't leave me alone to live my life in peace. Being a police officer, I knew that he would have the resources and proximity to control me.

In 2010, he resigned as a police officer, but the effects this occupation reaped on his psyche did not subside. The anxiety, the emotions, the hypervigilance and the aggression were all still there. He took a government contract job in Alabama, which gave me the breathing room I needed to move forward with separation. Initially, he accepted the decision, and I thought that we would move forward. He had people at my gym spy on me and report back about who I was speaking with, and where I would go during my free time.

His behavior ramped up exponentially through 2011. He called my cell and work phone incessantly. If I didn't pick up he would email or text until I would finally respond. He would use any tactic that would get a reaction. It ranged from being incredibly sweet to threatening to show up places and embarrassing me. I did my best to try to manage his behavior. My biggest concern was protecting the people in my life. I felt confident that I was "safe" from him, but I didn't trust him not to hurt those around me. During the summer of that year he began to show up at my house or places I was out. It was almost as though he had a tracking device on my phone or some informant in my close circle of my friends. It was hard to reconcile fiercely loving Marine and protective police officer I knew with the man who was becoming more and more of a threat.

I had someone at a police department give him a "courtesy" call in hopes of getting him to back off. I wanted to file a restraining order, but I knew that would impact his Top Secret clearance and taking away his livelihood would only push him closer to the edge.

By the time September 2011 rolled around I was bobbing and weaving, trying to scrape out a life outside of his stalking and harassment. I had resigned myself to exist until I could find a job far enough away that he couldn't get to me. I used to joke, in the sick way Marines do, that if I didn't make it to work on Monday that he killed me over the weekend.

I blocked his number so he couldn't call or text. His only form of communication was through email. On the 23rd I went out to dinner with my best friend and then home early. I had to CrossFit the next day, and my mom was visiting. The last email he sent me that night said, "I give you my word on every Marine I've ever known if you don't call me back this will end badly." I was already asleep, but this wasn't a new threat from him. I had become relatively numb at this point.

I woke up when my bedroom light was turned on. I jumped up quickly and herded him towards the stairs to get him outside. I had him near the door when my mother walked out to see what was going on. I told her that everything was fine, and that he and I would have a discussion outside. I stood on the front porch while we discussed his issue. The last thing I said to him was that we both deserved to be happy.

He grunted something in response and then pulled a Glock 9mm out of the front of his jeans. I knew that gun because he had gifted it to me one year for my birthday and had recently taken it from my house. I didn't really worry when he took it back, I figured it was another power play and not worth the fight.

When he pulled the gun, my instinct was to duck. In reality, it is impossible to "Matrix" a bullet, but you can possibly move more quickly than the person with the weapon. He fired two shots. The grouping (the distance between the bullets) was pretty damn good. The bullets struck me two inches apart, both at my neck. I could feel blood pouring down from my mouth as I fell to the ground, unable to move or scream. One bullet hit my carotid artery and then traveled down to collapse my lung and break my T-2 vertebrae, which caused me to be paralyzed. The other bullet went in behind my jaw and out through my front teeth.

Then he fired a third shot, and I knew he forfeited his life. Those years of constant exposure to trauma with no committed attempt to cope contorted a man who genuinely wanted to take care of everyone into a singularly focused shell of a person. He was kind, brave, and well loved by most people he met and he was clearly in pain. The VA deemed him 90% disabled with PTSD, and while they acknowledged the trauma in payment there wasn't a concerted effort to ensure that he was getting the help that he needed. He was not an anomaly, there are so many military personnel and law enforcement officers that struggle to balance both sides or their life, the warrior and the everyday human.

I'm grateful my mother was there to save me. She urgently tended to my wounds and pleaded for me not to leave her. She is one of the heroes of the story.

Life has been a steep uphill roll for me, living my new life as a paralyzed person. I hope that my story will inspire people to get the help that they need. For some it's counselling to battle the memories or trauma and for others it's the courage to recognize that their situation is unhealthy or dangerous. Life is worth it and you owe it to yourself to create the best one possible.

-(Fmr.) Staff Sergeant Erin Cobb

Chapter 4
You Can Have a Social Life Too!

We both know that police work can be more than a little draining, and since most of us are not riding a desk all day, it is nice to come home and vegetate when you have been out who knows where for who knows how many hours dealing with stuff.

But that does not mean that you do not need social interaction with friends like everyone else.

You do not have to go off on some epic adventure with a dozen friends every week, but simple little encounters with people you care about here and there can make a huge difference in terms of your mental and spiritual health. Let us take a closer look, shall we?

1. Real friends only!

It is simply imperative that you make sure not to surround yourself with people who do not allow you to be yourself. It is not that you need a ton of friends you have known for your whole life, because even a new friend has the choice to either respect your unique weirdness or alienate you for it.

If you are on the fence about a person as far as whether or not they will judge you, do not evaluate their behavior while you are hanging out, evaluate your own. That is where the answer to the question of being comfortable is. Can you be yourself around them or not? It is a fairly simple equation.

I hate to say it, but no matter how close the person is (even family), if they constantly criticize, mock, or otherwise threaten your ability to express yourself, then it is time to spend less time with that person. I am not saying you have to totally ghost them forever, but it would be wise that you surround yourself more closely with people who will respect you for who you are.

2. Limit your time around negative people

I use the word "limit" because I realize that everybody has at least one or more mandatory interactions a day with someone who spreads negative energy - or most days, at least.

Energy is everywhere, and it absolutely has an effect on our mental, physical, and spiritual wellbeing. If you hang around a gloomy group of people, then sure enough, that energy is going to rub off on you. If you hang around people who are always gossiping and trying to stir up trouble for no good reason, then once more, that might end up being you.

I will even admit that I get sucked into these pitfalls more often than I care to say, but it certainly does happen. The trick is having the presence of mind to realize it is happening, and step two is just like the heading says: limit your time around those negative energy spreaders.

One of the most common traits shared universally by successful people in all areas of achievement is the tendency to surround oneself with the right kind of people. I do not mean rich, hyper-intelligent, or well-connected people, but positive people. No matter what their status in life is, if they have nothing else but a positive attitude, then they will make a worthy friend.

3. Grow friendships outside of law enforcement

It is obviously a win-win in most cases, hanging out with the like-minded people you work with, or even other law enforcement officers you do not see on a daily basis, but that does not mean work friends should be your only friend group.

I say this for a couple reasons. First, in the context of law enforcement officers hanging out with each other, the conversation has a tendency to turn towards, well, the traumatic scenes those officers have been witness to or involved in. Add in a beer or two, and you will both be one-upping each other until you are thoroughly, thoroughly reliving the incidents in your mind.

Secondly, hanging out with people outside of law enforcement helps to broaden your perspective and switch things up in a number of ways. You get to hear different perspectives on issues that your department buddies may not have brought up, and most of all, you do not have to deal with the cycle of traumatic storytelling.

Plus, you can sarcastically mock your friend when they try to tell you just how world-ending Bob's typo on the excel spreadsheet was. "Yeah, that does sound pretty scary, good thing I just deal with violent criminals."

4. Turn your coworkers into real friends

We are relational beings. Humans were not meant to be alone, and when a law enforcement officer demonstrates asocial tendencies, the risks for depression and other mental health issues go up greatly. The same goes for non-police populations. The less time you spend interacting with people, the less effective you will be at getting information out of someone, de-escalating a situation, clearly explaining things, and many other vital skills required of an officer.

I am not saying that you should constantly harangue coworkers you barely know to hang out everyday with you. The chances are probably there that you spend time outside of work with a few coworkers whom you have grown tight with because of surviving dangerous encounters. Plus, just in general, having friends to hang out with at the end of a long week especially is very good for your mental fortitude. We all know that Monday morning (well, it is not necessarily Monday for all cops) sense of dread after a weekend. The more fulfilling and healthy your weekend socializing was, the less dread you will feel.

5. Join a group fitness gym

Yes, this of course has strong tie-ins to the physical wellbeing/exercise chapter we covered extensively earlier, but I am referring more to the social component of group fitness classes. The group fitness class setting is beneficial for two ways: one social and one productivity related.

First and foremost, when you sweat with folks once or a couple times a week for a couple months or more, you tend to talk before/after class and develop some friendships. This is the primary reason I am bringing up the whole concept of group gym classes again.

Secondly, nobody wants to look like a weenie and not keep up with everyone else in the class, so the group setting will encourage you to work harder and keep up.

The end result? You will be super fit, you will make new friends, and you will be better equipped to handle the stressors of your career in law enforcement.

6. Join a club or organization

Law enforcement as an occupation is fairly unique in that it exposes us to a very small percentage of the population, consisting of people who are often more than a little hard to work with.

If you do not spend some time with other, more well-adjusted subsets of the general population, you may fall down the toxic "us vs them" mentality rabbit hole, which I have seen more than once in plenty of officers. I do not mean to be petty for the sake of a joke, but honestly, this is unabomber-level thinking.

What I have found is that joining a club, team, or organization of some kind will help temper this sense of bitterness towards the public quite effectively. Rather than always dealing with that small, troubled percentage, you can join a community, church, or charity group - or whatever appeals to you. Just join something!

For example, Toastmasters is a great organization for anyone who wants to work on their public speaking skills. I am not saying you have to go in that specific direction, but it is highly applicable for law enforcement officers. Just an example for you to check out.

7. Put your family first

It may be a lighthearted joke on the surface, but it is unfortunately at least partially rooted in truth: Preachers' kids and cops' kids are the worst! I am not asserting that it is 100% true, but the fact that this saying exists points at a problem of accessibility.

Most of us are highly committed to our jobs, and some of us have to work crazy (long and/or sporadic) hours, which means that family time can often take a hit.

Jobs and schedule changes will come and go, but your family is your rock. It is your obligation to spend time with them, and if your schedule is crazy, that means making a few sacrifices in terms of your downtime - it is just the way this profession is.

I do not want to hear one more story about a marriage/family falling apart in a police family because the officer was not home enough for their spouse and their family. Even with our schedules, we are home enough to make family obligations work - we just have to, well, *make them work. If you can not make it work, then leaving the job does not make you weak and/or a failure.*

8. Parents! Do not stop going out on dates!

I realize that every parent says this, but it is a fundamental truth of parenthood: kids are just an absolute joy, and they change the way you see just about everything. They unlock a potential you did not know you had in terms of how much you could love another human being. They are God's gift to us, and it is a safe bet that every time you see a smile on their face, you feel like a million bucks.

Are...are they gone? Did they stop looking over your shoulder? Okay, now to the real point - my gosh, can kids sap your energy and time! I love them as much as the next parent, but law enforcement parents especially are often hard-pressed to just cover the basics, let alone work in some fun learning/enrichment/fun activities with their kids.

As I mentioned earlier, what may just be a natural rhythm for a typical 9-5 person, i.e., see your kids off before you leave in the morning, see them when you come home and hang out with them, etc., is not necessarily available to most police officers. You may have to actively invest more time a couple of days a week and then not see your kids at all on a couple other days. It is definitely tough, especially with little ones.

Take the time to keep that bond as strong as possible, not just for your kids, but for your spouse and your own happiness. They help hold a family together, so use that resource to keep yours strong.

9. Be willing to share your experiences with family and friends

As a rookie on the force, I initially thought that by telling my non-law-enforcement friends that I did not want to talk about the job with them, I was safeguarding my sanity. As it turns out, the exact opposite occurred. That was a mistake.

If you have experienced a traumatic event to the point where talking about it makes you feel like you are reliving it, then it is time to seek treatment. If that is not the case, then trust me, telling your stories can be very therapeutic as long as you do not wallow in self-pity or other negative thought patterns. It is all about how you interpret the event, not just the event itself.

Plus, your friends who are office workers cannot really compete with your level of crazy and exciting when it comes to on-the-job drama stories, so it is a great way to engage the people around you and build friendships. Just as long as you are not telling so many stories to an annoying level, and harming your own mental wellbeing.

If you refuse to open up to people at all, this practice will eventually manifest itself in one negative outcome or another. At the very least, tell the stories that do not bother you so much but are still amusing. Even rookies have at least a handful of those.

10. Drop the expectations and accept your company for who they are

I apologize if the title sounds a bit aggressive - that is not my intention. My point here was wisely passed on to me from a former pastor at my church, who, when referencing the stress and annoyance of family holiday get-togethers, gave me a singular piece of advice that still resonates with me today.

"Don't put expectations on people."

Everyone has that friend Bob, for example, who ties one on and gets loud and obnoxious. It could be three in the afternoon, and Bob would still be carrying on with all the grace and self-awareness of a bull in a China shop - yelling, laughing super loud, and so forth.

Each time you see him, you might think, "Okay, last time was probably just a fluke. I hope Bob controls himself a little bit more this time."

Sure enough, Bob does not. Because Bob is just doing Bob, and it is what it is. If you still enjoy hanging out with him and your mutual friends, then simply stop expecting Bob to act any other way. I am not saying you are not within your right to head to the other side of the room, ask your friend not to bring him along, or whatever else, but if he *does* show up, just let whatever happens happen. We have all been Bob on at least one occasion.

11. Manage/prevent your social media addiction

Allow me to offer some context to begin. A few years ago, I watched the well-known comic and actor *Aziz Ansari* talk about how people just simply do not meet up anymore. He blames social media for this disturbing trend, and I have to say, he makes a darn solid argument.

You will have to watch his entire routine for the "yuks", but even without the context of the rest of his act that day, he made a salient point that stuck with me. Social media creates a false sense of comfort. It makes us feel super popular and well-liked, but being popular on social media is far less rewarding than we give it credit for.

It is great to receive updates on your friends via social media, but we are now consuming this content to the extent where it artificially replaces our desire to physically hang out with said friends. Why would you when you can just check their social media to see how everything is going?

In the case of law enforcement, a group who deals regularly with the worst of society, nothing is more helpful in a social context than a face-to-face interaction with a decent, insightful, funny human being. Just make sure it is face-to-face.

12. Volunteer

"Dude, are you kidding me? I'm a cop?!"

I fully get it. You already do a lot for people that goes well beyond what you are paid to do. Still, joining a volunteer group can help you strengthen your connection with positive members of the community, get some much-needed exposure to non-criminals, and reinforce your love for serving others.

I used to volunteer for a particular NFL team's concession stands with my fellow Knights of Columbus, and when the orders piled up and the lines stretched around the stadium, we enjoyed yelling at each other (jokingly of course), "I need nachos! NOW!"

Through the awesome power of Google, you can easily find plenty of volunteer opportunities in your area. Just find something you like to do, or maybe even something you have never tried before, and give it a whirl. I have never shown up to a volunteer opportunity that I was not thanked profusely for. Volunteering is good and it feels good to make a difference!

13. Quality, not quantity

It is far better for you to have a small number of highly trustworthy, positive, and supportive friends, than to have a ton of acquaintances that you cannot confide in. It is kind of a tendency of police officers, I have noticed, to prefer smaller and more connected friend groups anyway, so let me just reassure you that this is more than okay. It is preferable, even.

Now, if you are the type of spontaneous and outgoing person that just loves to go out and talk to/meet all kinds of new people, please do not allow me to trample over that cool, charismatic personality you have got going on. I totally see the value in meeting a lot of people and making friends with whoever sits next to you.

The "but" here is that, while it is cool to be super outgoing and make a lot of acquaintances, just keep at least two or three friends who you can really confide in. You cannot really confide in the person that happens to also be a regular at Jo Schmo's neighborhood bar. I mean, you could, because it is a bar, but it would not be as fulfilling a conversation as it would if the other person really knew how to speak to your experiences and tendencies like a more trusted friend would.

Cheers?!

14. Listen

I am probably butchering the saying, but if you are always talking, you will never learn anything new. Guilty, I am. Excuse that Yoda diction. It goes without saying, some of us are just naturally predisposed to talk more than others, and that is totally okay. If neither you nor your friend know how to listen, however, then we can certainly run into trouble.

Listening is not just about you learning something new - it is about reciprocity. It is about letting your friend tell you a story, vent, explain something, or whatever else. Conversations involve two people, and the best ones allow for mutual give-and-take.

The next time you are talking with a friend, I encourage you to assess how much you actually listen. If you walk away from the conversation only thinking about what *you* said, and not what they said, then you have not learned much or allowed that friend to confide in you!

Plus, the more you listen to someone, the more you can help them in the future. That is what strong and productive friendships are built on: learning how the other person works so you can enrich their life by offering advice that speaks to their experiences and preferences.

15. Remember, you are off the clock. Let your guard down.

As police officers, we are trained to incisively analyze everything around us for safety purposes, including body language, suspicious behavior patterns, and so forth. To this day, my wife rolls her eyes at me when I make friends move to a different spot at the table when we are at a restaurant so I can see the main entrance.

However, I still do not act like I am at work, at least not completely, and I encourage you to avoid doing so as well.

Would you call your friend "sir" or "ma'am," or answer their question with "affirmative"? I highly doubt it (and if that is just your personality, no offense!). It is vital that you turn off the police shtick when you are not on the clock, for a number of reasons. First and foremost, it is a vital piece of that "you're not endangered anymore, brain, you can rest and digest now" formula we have been talking about.

Letting your guard down *some* is also important, but if you roll up to the restaurant or wherever else in tactical pants and a blue line shirt, you are cueing your mind to stay in work mode. Nowadays, you are also making yourself a target. I am not implying you are scared, I am just saying that even subtle habits here and there can prevent you from de-stressing like you are supposed to after work.

16. Never forget the impact that other people have on you

I wrote more extensively in "*Mental Health Fight of the Heroes in Blue*" about the causes and detrimental effects of asocial and avoidance behaviors that often stem from chronic stress and traumatic incidents when it comes to law enforcement officers.

When I came back from Iraq, I did not have any interest in taking a vacation to the beach with my friends. Why? The thought of the sand alone triggered a wave of negative emotions and traumatic memories that I wanted to avoid at all costs.

But then I thought to myself, *Why did I do that?* The beach is a great place to vacation, and friends make it all the more so. Policing is no different than military service in this respect. Maybe you had to discharge your firearm in defense of your own or another person's life, and now your brain uses avoidance behaviors as a "coping mechanism."

In reality, this is an asocial/avoidance behavior, and it can alienate you from your friends. The longer you stay alienated, the less you benefit from those crucial friendships. I am not saying you should go through absolute torment just to spend a few hours with your buddies. When you feel even remotely up to it, successfully confronting and overcoming one trigger at a time for your social life's sake is an incredible feeling. Trust me.

17. Avoid being dull!

Remember #14? Ironically, if you do not, I *know* you need to review it again, because that was the point about listening. Well, on the flip side of listening is contributing to the conversation, of course, and my question to you is, what are you bringing to the table?

I am not saying you have to have these awesome stories of this enchanted life of adventure and intrigue to unload on someone, but even the most mundane of conversations can be delivered in a way that stimulates interest.

After all, you are trained in reading nonverbal cues anyway, so if you are indeed boring someone to death, you should be able to pick that up pretty quickly.

I am not advocating that you try to be someone else. We all have interesting, thought-provoking, and hilarious thoughts and ideas we would like to share with the world. Some of us hold back for fear of being laughed at or misunderstood. Rather than trying to be someone else, then, just get those inhibitions out of the way, dismiss with the small talk, and say something *really* compelling.

18. Acknowledge similarities between yourself and your friends

According to best-selling author and behavioral science expert *Vanessa Van Edwards,* finding common ground with someone else, even if they are not a super close friend, can be very socially gratifying. For example, "Hey, you like Star Wars? I like Star Wars too!"

Now, that is not a very tough one, but the more specific or obscure the commonality is, the more rewarding it can be. It is funny how something as random as a cosmic coincidence (like growing up on the same street as an old friend and not knowing it) can strengthen a friendship, but it just does.

Conversely, if you spend a lot of energy just naming off the many ways in which you and the other person are different, you may end up alienating them. Both concepts require a balance, of course. It is cool to meet someone who sees things from a different perspective, but not if they are so far out of your element that you cannot even agree on the most basic of points.

In fact, I encourage you to try this technique out during an encounter with a citizen on your next call, traffic stop, or other interaction. Try it and see what it does for the tension. If you see something you can relate to on the person's shirt, a team logo on a hat, a bumper sticker or whatever else, then make mention of whatever the common ground is. We deal with a lot of frustrated people, and you would be amazed at how this technique can diffuse a lot of this frustrated energy.

19. Have friends in different areas

Balance is a tricky concept to master in many areas, but it is especially elusive when it comes to our social wellbeing. Finding someone who is different enough to offer advice and support you while being similar enough to understand your viewpoints and agree with you often is harder than we think.

Remember the show *Friends?* Of course you do - it is Friends. Even if you did not watch it, you were probably vaguely aware that the characters all hung out with each other at the same coffee shop, sitting in the same spots on the same sofa and chairs every single time. That is not exactly mixing it up in the friends department.

Lifespan psychology expert *Amanda Hawthorn* put it best when it comes to this idea, saying:

"Rather than having to rely on one group of friends for all your socializing, having multiple groups of friends will ensure you are never at a loss for things to do or people to do them with."

20. Socializing contributes to longevity

In all fairness, I will admit this is more of a factoid than an actionable "tip," but I had to sneak in this anecdote because it bears so much importance to the topic.

I have got one personal example that social well being affects physical wellbeing, and it involves my grandmother. This woman is 93 years old and as sharp as ever. Know why that is? I have got my money on the fact that she drives to the Senior Citizen's Center and has a blast with her friends all the time. Many of her friends are about as old as she is, and they all support each other in this way.

There is a big difference between living and not dying. We can spend too much time as law enforcement officers worrying about not dying. Sure we can keep worrying about that, on some level, because it helps us make smart decisions. What we really need to worry about is livelihood

- living longer, more fulfilled lives. And that means connecting with friends, whether you are 39 or 93.

21. Remember acknowledging similarities? Now, seek them out!

I know I may sound a little self-contradictory here, since I have encouraged you at multiple points to hang out with people *outside* of your normal law enforcement officer type, but that does not mean the practice is exclusive. It is still important to find people who are like you and spend some time with them.

Besides, the commonality you are looking for does not have to necessarily do with law enforcement. You have other interests and hobbies, right? Seek out people with the same interests and hobbies to make new friends that you will never run out of things to do with.

For example, you can hang out at a sports bar or restaurant where you know there will be fellow fans of your favorite team. Or, if you are a parent and you live in a neighborhood that has kid-friendly events (typically put on by the homeowners association), then make your way over, meet some fun parents, and watch those little anarchists run around all off balance because of their disproportionate head-size-to-body ratio. Always a good time.

22. Get a dog

If this is completely out of the question for whatever reason, then I encourage you to make your way over to #23. If you are still here, then let us talk about a good, sociable, active dog. Dogs are not only therapeutic in their own right, but they are also an easy way to connect with people in your area and make new friends.

Again, this harkens back to the idea of commonality being the driving force for friendships. People are ironically more willing to ask about the dog you are walking before they ask about you. You might initiate the conversation or your dog might, either way it is an all-around great way to meet new people.

Plus, you get to play with an awesome furball, love/feed/nurture a creature that depends on you, and go outside more! Dogs are like walking antidepressants, when you really think about it.

23. Make friends with people who disagree with you

Obviously, similarities are very helpful in laying the groundwork for a solid friendship, being *too* much like each other can have its drawbacks. Sometimes, in fact, the most rewarding discussions between friends come from debates and disagreements. It stimulates both parties to think creatively as they try to express their point differently and empathize with the other person. Debate is just a healthy tool for many reasons.

This is not to say that you should practice the whiny, overly sarcastic arguing styles like those of the social media sphere. (Is it just me, or does it seem like everyone is so polarized and upset nowadays?) The point of a disagreement is not to get the other side to think how you think, or to show them how "dumb" they are, but to produce your point in the best way possible so that they may **reconsider** how they think or **enrich** their current understanding of the debate topic with new information.

If you just try to "win," you will never win. If you try to contribute insight that could change someone's life for the better, then congratulations - you know how to disagree with someone like an adult.

I feel like now more than ever, the world needs to adopt these mantras.

It is okay if someone disagrees with you. That is their choice.

Just because you think you are right, does not mean you are.

You can still be friends with someone who disagrees with you.

24. "You can make more friends in two months by becoming interested in other people than you can in two years by trying to get other people interested in you.
-Dale Carnegie

Mic drop - I'm out! No really, that is one of my favorite quotes of all time, and for good reason. What Carnegie was getting at in his famous book entitled *How to Win Friends and Influence People* falls really closely in line with what I said about listening. We are all really good at talking ourselves up and sharing our stories, so when people are actually good listeners (instead of just talking back at us and interrupting us), we glue onto them like mollusks. We want people to be interested in us because it feeds our egos. Plain and simple.

Essentially, the fact that this quote is true represents a strong bias in the economy of conversation we find ourselves in: there is a low supply and high demand for listeners, and vice versa for talkers.

And do not dare pull that "Meh, people are exhausting and everyone is terrible now. I just want to watch TV anyway."

Where do you think you gained that skewed worldview in the first place? The TV! And around and around the cycle goes.

25. Nobody makes it out of this life alive. Go have fun.

Think about the irony of it all. When we were young children, we were told not to talk to strangers. What is interesting is when the you-know-what really hits the fan, we dial up a complete stranger, i.e., you as the police officer, to come bail us out of a terrible situation.

What you do next can determine whether or not you end up making an impact on that person's life for the better. In the process of helping people out as were called to do, we endure a lot of frustrating, boring, and even traumatic experiences that can seriously affect all aspects of our wellbeing: physical, mental, social, and spiritual. This is what leads to depression, anxiety, addictions, and so on and so forth.

I do not mean to diminish the importance of my own work here, but I suppose what I am trying to say with this last point is that, if you are too worried about being healthy, then *that worry* will become a new stressor that actually makes you less healthy.

In other words, temper your efforts towards physical, mental, social, and spiritual wellbeing with a bit of fun. Pick a time to do less analyzing. Less worrying. Just relax for a minute and do something spontaneous. It is called fun. We all deserve it.

Let Us Wrap This Up

As Louis Feliz wrote in _Leveraging Anxiety: Fights Within Our Darkest Moments,_ knowledge alone is not power. Hopefully you felt that this content related to you, but whether it did or not, you cannot make a definitive change if you do not apply the knowledge. We have to bridge that gap between "hm, that sounds cool," and "yes, I'll do that tomorrow at 6 AM and see how it goes."

All of these techniques, from getting the proper nutrition to working on your social life, require action, commitment, and change. Oh, that is right - I forgot #101! Here it is: **Care for yourself, and you can care for others.**

You were not blessed with the gift of life so you could do nothing with it. You were not sworn in as a police officer so you could sit idly while there are people out there who need help. You were made to protect and help others, and you maximize your potential in this area when you take care of yourself first. The voice that compels you to take care of others is already there. You just need to look out for yourself as well.

As much as I wanted to take a more lighthearted approach with this book, I simply cannot fail to address the reality of the situation in terms of the mental health of police officers. The past three years have been hell for officers, so says the numbers, as the number of officer suicides exceeded on-duty deaths. It is also a difficult time to be an officer, especially a good one, because the world has seen the worst of us. The tiny minority of officers who go off the rails, such as publicly dehumanizing George Floyd and killing

Walter Scott, have soured the barrel as far as many people are concerned.

But this equation can and will change. It has to change. And it starts with taking care of yourself, daily.

References

About Vanessa Van Edwards. (n.d.). Science of people. https://www.scienceofpeople.com/about/

American Osteopathic Association. (n.d.). The benefits of yoga. https://osteopathic.org/what-is-osteopathic-medicine/benefits-of-yoga/

Better Health Channel. (n.d.). Walking for good health. State Government of Victoria, Australia Department of Health & Human Services. https://www.betterhealth.vic.gov.au/health/healthyliving/walking-for-good-health

Brown, J. J. (2018, January 5). 8 surprising health benefits of B vitamins. Everyday Health. https://www.everydayhealth.com/pictures/surprising-health-benefits-b-vitamins/

Burgin, T. (n.d.). History of yoga. YogaBasics. https://www.yogabasics.com/learn/history-of-yoga/

Butler, S. (n.d.). The importance of spinal health. The Joint Chiropractic. https://www.thejoint.com/california/los-angeles/midtown-crossing-31160/194942-importance-spinal-health

Carnegie, D. (1936). How to win friends and influence people. Simon & Schuster.

DeLauer, D. (2019, September 25). Elderberry vs. illness - Does it help? [Video]. YouTube. https://www.youtube.com/watch?v=ggckX7Gsgsw

Dispenza, J. (2013). Breaking the habit of being yourself: how to lose your mind and create a new one. Hay House Inc.

Edberg, H. (2015, March 6). How to improve your social life: 6 of my favorite timeless tips. The Positivity Blog. https://www.positivityblog.com/how-to-improve-your-social-life/

Eker, T. H. (2005). Secrets of the millionaire mind: Mastering the inner game of wealth. Harper Business.

Feliz, L. R. (2019). Leveraging anxiety: Gifts within our darkest moments. (n.p).

Harvard Health Publishing (2020, July 6). Relaxation techniques: Breath control helps quell errant stress response. https://www.health.harvard.edu/mind-and-mood/relaxation-techniques-breath-control-helps-quell-errant-stress-response

Haworth, A. (2018, March 31). 3 steps to improve your social life. SocialPro. https://socialpronow.com/blog/best-ways-improve-social-life/

HeadsUpGuys. (n.d.). Social life and depression. https://headsupguys.org/practical-tips/social-life/

Hof, W. (n.d.). Home [YouTube channel]. YouTube. Retrieved August 4, 2020, from https://www.youtube.com/user/wimhof1/featured

Jennings, K. (2017, April 8). 9 impressive health benefits of chlorella. Healthline. https://www.healthline.com/nutrition/benefits-of-chlorella

Kirby, S. (2020, May 14). Is there a connection between caffeine and anxiety?. BetterHelp. https://www.betterhelp.com/advice/anxiety/is-there-a-connection-between-caffeine-and-anxiety/?utm_source=AdWords&utm_medium=Search_PPC_c&utm_term=_b&utm_content=77548444015&network=g&placement=&target=&matchtype=b&utm_campaign=6459244691&ad_type=text&adposition=&gclid=CjwKCAjw57b3BRBlEiwA1ImyttwfB76xdWSMrIHcyLEjcPHpkR0Oh5bHxgqk7CzWu6vjZ1ty_P3TBRoCVXgQAvD_BwE

Link, R. (2019, March 1). Spinach vs. kale: Is one healthier?. Healthline. https://www.healthline.com/nutrition/kale-vs-spinach

McCulloch, M. (2018, October 11). 15 healthy foods high in B vitamins. Healthline. https://www.healthline.com/nutrition/vitamin-b-foods

Mental Health Foundation (n.d.). Alcohol and mental health. https://www.mentalhealth.org.uk/a-to-z/a/alcohol-and-mental-health#:~:text=One of the main problems,a key chemical in depression.

Miller, K. (2015, August 20). Can what you eat affect your mental health? WebMD. https://www.webmd.com/mental-health/news/20150820/food-mental-health#1

Mylett, E. (2018). Max out your life. Jetlaunch.

Neuronation. (n.d.). Why you need to smile more. https://blog.neuronation.com/en/why-you-need-to-smile-more

New International Bible. (2011). Bible Gateway. https://www.biblegateway.com (Original work published 1978).

Paddock, C. (2013, June 20). Silver boosts effect of antibiotics. Medical News Today. https://www.medicalnewstoday.com/articles/262290#1

Parachin, V. M. (2020, January 12). 21 ways to build a stronger spiritual life. Vibrant Life. http://www.vibrantlife.com/21-ways-to-build-a-stronger-spiritual-life/

Richtmyer, P. W., & Brink, W. (2018, September 4). The patrol athlete. POLICE Magazine. https://www.policemag.com/342553/the-patrol-athlete

Schlimm, J. (2017, December 6). Smile! (even when you don't feel like it). HuffPost. https://www.huffpost.com/entry/smile-even-when-you-dont-_b_8782164?guccounter=1&guce_referrer=aHR0cHM6Ly93d3cuZ29vZ2xlLmNvbS8&guce_referrer_sig=AQAAAB18ZKOHX4h4uJXg61HH4HtZiOE43ddMOZazxlmrv9IH29mgMfGM8eTKZW2oVl6v050jQYoM96PQUqjhHT_m7ASLCJu4eOHuDtT0tHOGQSzlw3sTwKz5ctfRDbb0nOLIn4uSOnrdFq7pH8laOPvKpMe_k8cI92-GWlfft4O1al3w

Study Finds. (2018, December 20). Survey: 1 in 4 adults checks phone less than a minute after waking up. https://www.studyfinds.org/survey-quarter-checks-phones-less-than-minute-after-waking/

Swansea Illinois (n.d.). A police officer's prayer.
    https://swanseail.org/2252/Police-Officers-
    Prayer#:~:text=Oh Almighty God%2C&text=Watch
    Over All Policemen and,Robberies%2C Riots%2C
    and Violence

Tejada, C. (2019, December 12). Why your phone shouldn't
    be a part of your morning routine. HuffPost.
    https://www.huffingtonpost.ca/entry/dont-check-
    phone-in-
    morning_ca_5df24c1ae4b01e0f295b6d0a#:~:text=A
    study from IDC Research,of waking up each morning.

Tracy, B. (2011). No excuses!: The power of self-discipline.
    Vanguard Press.

Ware, M. (2019, November 7). What are the health benefits
    of vitamin D? Medical News Today.
    https://www.medicalnewstoday.com/articles/161618

WebMD. (2019, June 18). Surprising reasons to get more
    sleep. https://www.webmd.com/sleep-
    disorders/benefits-sleep-more

WebMD. (n.d.). Zinc.
    https://www.webmd.com/vitamins/ai/ingredientmono
    -982/zinc

Zelman, K. M. (2010, January 7). The benefits of vitamin C.
    WebMD. https://www.webmd.com/diet/features/the-
    benefits-of-vitamin-c#1.

Made in the USA
Coppell, TX
12 March 2025

47028924R00066